Jesuit Lives through the Ages

WITH CHRIST IN SERVICE

Edited by Patrick Carberry SJ

Published by Messenger Publications, 2017

ISBN 978 1 910248 70 6

Designed by Messenger Publications Design Department
Typeset in Adobe Caslon Pro
Printed by Johnswood Press Ltd.

Messenger Publications,
37 Lower Leeson Street, Dublin D02 W938
www.messenger.ie

CONTENTS

Part Three: To the ends of the Earth

FOREWORD

'We are not monks', said Jerónimo Nadal, who in 1553 was sent by St Ignatius to introduce the constitutions to the young Jesuit recruits in Spain and Portugal. 'The world is our cloister', he explained. 'The world is our house'. From the very beginning, the Jesuits were meant to be outward-bound, to be engaged with the world in all its variety, to be mobile and even restless in service of the Lord and his people. Flexibility and availability for mission were to be among their chief characteristics.

The needs of our world have remained the inspiration of the Jesuits down through the ages. In the unpredictable circumstances of time and place, Jesuits have been challenged to respond in concrete fashion to the realities of the day. The sixteen stories told in this book are inspiring examples of this Jesuit characteristic. No two stories are the same, because times and places are different and need different responses. Yet each one has a common inspiration: to bring the consolation of the gospel to people greatly in need of it.

In our own day, we Jesuits are once again attempting to respond to the challenges of our times. More than ever, perhaps, in this age of rapid change, we need to be creative, flexible and available to go wherever the road takes us. More than ever, too, we know that we must not travel alone if our mission is to be to be effective. We need to work alongside generous people – whether lay, religious or priests – in a real sharing partnership. Above all, we need to have the wisdom to know that, while we do the sowing, it is the Lord alone who produces the harvest.

Leonard Moloney SJ
Provincial of the Irish Jesuits

Part One

Beginnings

May Christ deign to be favourable to these our tender beginnings.
(Formula of the Institute 9)

~ 1 ~

Ignatius Loyola (1491–1556)

Patrick Carberry SJ

> Try to keep your soul always in peace and quiet,
> always ready for whatever our Lord may wish to
> work in you. It is certainly a higher virtue of the soul,
> and a greater grace, to be able to enjoy the Lord in
> different times and different places than in only one.
>
>   – Ignatius Loyola

The sixteenth century in Europe was a time of rapid change. Unimaginable discoveries were being reported from distant places. New ideas, rooted in classical antiquity, were spreading from Italy, transforming the very assumptions that underpinned people's lives. Stories of religious insubordination were filtering through from the north. The world was becoming an unfamiliar place.

Ambitious Youth

Rumours of these developments would have reached the Loyola household from time to time, but they probably had little impact on life there during Ignatius's early years, for he lived in a place largely untouched by the outside world. Tucked away in their modest castle in the remote Basque region of Spain, the Loyolas were a family of minor nobility. Ignatius – or Iñigo, to give him his baptismal name – was the youngest of thirteen children. Following a basic education, he spent the years of his early adulthood (1507–21) as a courtier in the household of the royal treasurer and, later, in the service of the Duke of Nájera. His ambition was to become a knight one day, like the heroes of old whom he liked to read about in the popular romances of the time.

Preparation for this privileged way of life was arduous. It involved extensive training in horsemanship, archery, swordsmanship and the tactics of warfare, as well as learning the strict etiquette of courtly life. Ignatius committed himself wholeheartedly to the task, satisfied with nothing less than excellence. In his spare time he enjoyed jousting, carousing and dancing. Although small in stature, he was well built and, knowing that he was attractive to women, he dressed smartly in tight-filling hose and doublet. He was also haughty and arrogant, and from time to time he became embroiled in violent skirmishes. On one occasion he was charged with a serious offence before the law. What this offence was we are not certain, but he only managed to escape conviction on a technicality.

Radical Transformation

The story of Ignatius's transformation from ambitious knight to penitent beggar is well known. In the region of Navarre, south of the Pyrenees, tensions had been growing between France and Spain, and in 1521 the French attacked the city of Pamplona. Foremost among its defenders was Ignatius. At his insistence, the Spaniards continued defending the fortress against the vastly superior enemy forces. It was only when Ignatius was disabled by a cannonball, severely injuring his right knee, that the Spaniards offered to surrender.

The victorious French carried Ignatius to their camp, where they treated him with courtesy and attended to his wounds before returning him to his family a very ill man. In Loyola, it was discovered that his knee had been badly set, however, and it was found necessary to break it again and reset it. As this was happening, Ignatius began to grow weaker. His health deteriorated alarmingly, and he was eventually advised to prepare for death. Then, against all odds, his condition improved. As he began to regain his strength he was shocked to notice that a bone below his knee was protruding in an ugly manner. Thinking, no doubt, of the fancy hose he would be wearing in court, he asked that the offending piece be cut away. Although he was warned that this would be more painful than anything he had so far suffered, he still persisted. He endured all this butchery, carried out without an anaesthetic, as only a truly heroic knight would: without showing any sign of pain other than to clench his fist, as he himself attests.

Even after the worst was over, Ignatius was confined to bed for several more months because another problem had been identified. One leg was found to be shorter than the other – a severe handicap for a would-be knight – and attempts were made to stretch it by hanging weights from it. Left alone with nothing but the nagging pain and his own thoughts, Ignatius found the days endless. In the absence of more exciting reading, he had to make do with the only two books available: *The Life of Christ* by Ludolph of Saxony and a volume containing stories of the saints' lives. Despite his initial reluctance, Ignatius found himself drawn imaginatively to what he was reading. In the quiet of his sickroom, he began to envisage the possibility of committing himself to a totally new way of life, in the service of a different master. If Francis could do it, he wondered, and if Dominic could do it, why couldn't he? Yet, he was torn. When not thinking of imitating the saints, he found himself fantasising about a certain lady he longed to impress and win for himself by poetic outpourings and feats of arms. Both attractions were strong; which could he trust?

Gradually, Ignatius became aware of different reactions within himself. When thinking of the lady he hoped to woo, he experienced great satisfaction at the time, but afterwards he felt dull and empty. On the other hand, thoughts of following Jesus not only brought him joy at the time, but long after the thoughts themselves had ceased he could feel lingering traces of that joy. He began to see that some attractions had an enduring quality about them, while others lacked any real depth. He began to realise, as he says in his memoir, 'that some thoughts left him sad and others happy'. It was his first exercise in the discernment of spirits.

A Different Path

By the time he left Loyola in 1522, Ignatius had determined to turn his back irrevocably on his past life and commit himself to the following of Jesus. He wasn't sure what that might involve, except that he wanted to go to Jerusalem as a beggar. To satisfy his concerned family, he reluctantly accepted the mule they offered him and set out on the long trek eastward towards Barcelona. On the way, he arrived at the Benedictine monastery of Montserrat, where he made a lengthy confession to one of the monks, gave away his fine clothes in exchange for a rough pilgrim's garment and abandoned his mule into the care of the monastery. Without prestige or money, he was now truly a beggar, limping his way through the Catalan countryside.

Shortly after Montserrat, Ignatius arrived in the small town of Manresa, where he interrupted his journey for ten months. There he was given a room in a hospice and, later, in the Dominican priory, but he spent much of his time, when not begging, in prayer and penance in a small cave nearby. Despite his sincere confession in Montserrat, Ignatius soon found himself tormented by remorse at his previously dissolute life and, unable to shake off these thoughts, he entered a phase of bitter scruples. Unable to find any peace, and being close to despair, at one point he even contemplated suicide. And then, something happened! Sifting through his moods and feelings, he began to see that his ceaseless fretting over the past was prompted not by God, but by 'the enemy of our human nature'. It was another moment of discernment, and it awoke him from his anxiety 'as if from a dream'.

A Vision Shared

Freed from his obsession, Ignatius found himself flooded with light and joy once again. His previous torment was now replaced by extraordinary mystical experiences of the kind that would recur for the rest of his life. In recounting these events in later years, Ignatius emphasised how they helped him to see the world and his faith in a new way: 'The eyes of his understanding began to be opened', he says, and he viewed everything afresh 'with interior eyes'. God, he believed, was teaching him like a patient schoolmaster might teach a recalcitrant child, leading him to a totally new appreciation of the Blessed Trinity, the Incarnation, the Eucharist and how God is present in the whole of created reality. Aware of the precious nature of these gifts, Ignatius began to note down what he was learning and how God was teaching him.

Inevitably, in this small town, the new beggar became a source of curiosity. Though beggars were not uncommon, there was something about this one that made him different. He was said to pray for hours on end, and it was known that at the end of each day he gave away anything he had left over. While most of the time he said little, he listened with complete attention when anyone talked to him, and when he did speak his words had a strange power to move the heart. It wasn't long before local people began to come to him, pouring out their souls and seeking his guidance. Ignatius soon discovered that the jottings he had made of his own spiritual experiences were helpful for other people also, and he began to gather these jottings together in a more orderly fashion. Many years later, following much revision and many additions, they would become known as *The Spiritual Exercises*.

By the time he left Manresa, ten months after his arrival, Ignatius had begun to modify his unkempt appearance, in order to be more approachable to people coming for his help. While continuing to beg as before, and still on his way to Jerusalem, his hopes were now becoming clearer: he wanted 'to help souls', as he put it himself. Indeed, 'helping souls', in the most inclusive meaning of the words, would increasingly become the guiding principle of his life.

Another Beginning

From Barcelona, Ignatius crossed to Rome, and from there he went north to Venice, the gateway to the Holy Land. Having arrived by ship in Jaffa, his first sight of Jerusalem brought him 'a joy that did not seem natural', and as he later visited each of the holy places that same intense joy was renewed. It was Ignatius's intention to remain in the Holy Land, but when he mentioned this to the Franciscans, who were the guardians of the holy places, they demurred. The Provincial explained that life in the Holy Land was dangerous and that the friars couldn't assume responsibility for his safety. Ignatius replied that he was unafraid of imprisonment or death, and that he intended to stay. Exasperated, the Provincial warned him that he had the power to excommunicate anyone who refused to obey his orders. Such a prospect was too much for Ignatius, and he agreed to leave.

Bitterly disappointed, Ignatius set sail for Venice once again, trying to figure out where God was now leading him. His desire to 'help souls' was growing stronger all the time, but as he reflected on his experience he became aware of a serious inadequacy in himself. Despite the extraordinary illuminations he had received in Manresa, he realised that he had only a limited grasp of ordinary human learning and little ease of expression. To be truly effective, he decided, he needed to address this lack. And so began, at the age of thirty-three, a new phase of his life that would last for another eleven years: that of a student.

The Middle-Aged Student

Back in Barcelona in 1524, Ignatius enrolled in a class of young boys studying Latin. It must have been a strange sight, this grown man in beggar's clothes, his hair already receding, conjugating verbs and declining nouns in a class of youngsters. Not surprisingly, study didn't come easily to him, and Ignatius found himself frequently drawn away from the boring lessons by lofty spiritual thoughts and moving insights. Reflecting afterwards on these experiences, however, he came to the conclusion that if God wanted him to study Latin, such distractions, despite their appearance, could not also be from God. Acting on this moment of discernment, he approached his teacher, promising never to let his attention wander in this way again. From then on the temptations ceased.

After two years in Barcelona, Ignatius was ready for his university studies, but once again his plans were thwarted. First in Alcalá and later in Salamanca, Ignatius tried to settle down to the undergraduate regime, but without success. In both places, he found the programme somewhat chaotic and unstructured, and instead of studying he spent much time in spiritual conversations and teaching Christian doctrine at street corners, sometimes to large groups. Inevitably, these activities attracted the attention of the Inquisition, who wondered about the credentials of this uneducated layman, and suspected him of heresy. After imprisonment and interrogation, and following scrutiny of his *Spiritual Exercises,* he was cleared of any suspicion but, in each case, restrictions were imposed on his freedom to speak on matters of faith. Ignatius decided it was time to make a fresh start, this time in the premier university of its day, the Sorbonne in Paris.

Ignatius spent seven years at the University of Paris (1528–35), where he found the structured approach to learning suited him well. To concentrate better on his studies, he modified his begging habits and was more selective in 'helping souls'. In the Collège Sainte-Barbe, he shared a room with two other students: Francis Xavier, a Basque like himself, and Pierre Favre, from Savoy in France. Favre was a gentle soul, insecure and scrupulous, and he and Ignatius quickly warmed to each other. Xavier was different. Fiery and ambitious, he was initially suspicious of this reformed knight with his radical views, but eventually he too fell under the spell of Ignatius. All three are now saints.

As before, Ignatius's radical lifestyle and teaching aroused controversy and opposition in Paris, both among the staff and students. He was determined this time, however, that he would not be distracted from his studies, and in 1534 he was awarded the prestigious degree of Master of Arts. More significantly, during his years in Paris a small group of students, beginning with Favre and Xavier, gathered around him and began to form a loose association of like-minded friends. They all made the *Spiritual Exercises* at different times, and on 15 August 1534, the seven of them gathered for Mass in the little church of Saint Denis in Montmartre, then a small village just outside Paris. The celebrant was the newly ordained Pierre Favre, the first priest among them. As Favre held up the host at communion, each of them in turn committed himself by vow to a life of poverty, and to go on pilgrimage to Jerusalem. They added a qualification, however: if after a year's wait in Venice it proved impossible to depart for the Holy Land, they would instead go to Rome and put themselves at the service of the Pope for him to send them wherever he wished.

Varied Fortunes in Rome
After a visit to Loyola, undertaken on his doctor's advice, Ignatius set off for Venice, where the companions had arranged to gather in the hope of setting sail for the Holy Land. The little group, which now included three new members, spent their time in prayer, looking after the sick and abandoned, giving spiritual direction and preaching at street corners. For Ignatius this was a time of profound happiness, when he experienced a return of the most fervent consolation. It was also during this time that he was ordained priest, along with several of the others.

Unable to find a ship that would take them to the Holy Land, in 1537 Ignatius and his companions set out for Rome, as planned, to put themselves at the service of the Pope. On the way, they paused to pray in a small church at La Storta, on the outskirts of Rome. There Ignatius had a vision which he understood to be God's response to his deepest desire from the time of his conversion. He understood in a definitive way 'that God had placed him with his Son' as his companion and fellow-worker, and that God would be favourable to the little band in Rome. Strengthened by this renewed conviction, he and his companions arrived at their destination.

When they reached Rome, the reputation of the group as 'reformed priests' had gone before them, and the Pope welcomed them warmly. With their prestigious degrees from the University of Paris, he authorised them to teach theology in the university, as well as to hear confessions and preach in the city's churches. As before, they had special concern for those on the margins of society, including orphans, prostitutes and victims of the plague. 'Helping souls' meant caring for the whole person. All seemed to be going smoothly when, once again, suspicions and slander threatened to undermine their work. Rumours circulated – the most vicious so far – that Ignatius had been condemned by the Inquisition in Spain and Paris, and that he was a Lutheran in disguise. Ignatius faced the slander head-on. In an audience with the Pope, he gave him a detailed account of all the investigations that had been carried out, and reported the positive outcome in each case. He proposed that an independent judge be appointed to hold an enquiry into the charges, the findings of which would be fully respected. The Pope agreed. A tribunal was established, witnesses called, and Ignatius and his followers were completely exonerated.

A Vision Enshrined

A different kind of crisis was now looming on the horizon, however. In 1539, in response to persistent demands from various places, the Pope asked that two of the group be sent to Siena to help with the reform of the Church. Until then, they had never considered that their little band might be dispersed. Now they had to face the question of their future. If they were to be scattered in different places, should they attempt to remain united as a body, or should they simply go their separate ways? They quickly answered this question in favour of remaining together. This initial decision gave rise to innumerable other questions, and for three months they engaged in extended prayer and reflection about their future, meeting almost daily to address the sometimes complex issues that arose.

At the end of the three months, they arrived at a conclusion they had never consciously anticipated. They were proposing to establish a new religious order, one which in many respects would be radically different from any other. They drew up the outlines of this new order in a document known as *The Formula of the Institute*, and presented it to Pope Paul III who was initially favourable to the idea. However, it was met with strong opposition from many influential cardinals, who argued against the need for any new religious order. 'Let them join the Benedictines,' some said, 'or the Dominicans or the Franciscans.' Fearful for the future of the group, and anxious to preserve their integrity, Ignatius requested unremitting prayers as they awaited a response. Eventually, in September 1540, the Society of Jesus was formally approved.

Having spent the previous eighteen years free to wander the roads of Europe, Ignatius's world was now reduced to three small rooms in the centre of Rome. Elected General by his companions, it was there that he prayed for several hours each day and celebrated Mass. It was there too that he monitored the acceptance of new recruits and made decisions about their formation, life and the mission. From there he wrote innumerable letters – hundreds of them are still extant – and authorised a new and daring educational project that would eventually encompass the whole world. As a lasting legacy, he drew up in *The Constitutions of the Society of Jesus* a 'way of proceeding' that would endure through the centuries and keep his followers united in heart and mind, even though separated by time, place and occupation. By the end of his life, the lone beggar had become the leader of a thousand-strong movement reaching into every corner of the known world.

A Lasting Legacy

Who was Ignatius Loyola? It has often been tempting to reduce his life to a single, simplistic narrative, but such an interpretation clearly fails to do justice to this complex personality. He was a man of many parts, yet intensely focused on a single goal. He always remained something of the knight, eager to do great deeds for his Lord and Master. He never ceased to be the penitent beggar, wary of setting his heart on false securities of any kind. He was the mystic who frequently wept tears of consolation at prayer and during Mass. He was the spiritual guide who had such insight into people that 'he almost seemed to enter into their mind and heart', as one companion testified. He was committed to serious study and solid learning, insisting on the necessity of a scholarly basis for effective ministry. He was an inspirational leader, a daring innovator and an efficient administrator, one who consistently won the affection and trust of his followers.

So, who was he really? In the end, perhaps his own description of himself in his memoir is the only adequate one. There he calls himself 'the pilgrim'. Like any pilgrim, he had a goal in view – in his case to share with Jesus in his mission to the world – but how he was to achieve that goal was only revealed over time. Initially, he thought it would be in Jerusalem, but that wasn't to be. Over and over again, as if entering unknown terrain, the pilgrim had to change his plans, make adjustments, accept disappointments and failures, struggle with opposition and misunderstanding and set himself new courses. He had to learn to read the signs of the times, to listen to the movements of his own heart and to make choices – both big and small – that were consonant with his ultimate goal.

Ignatius learned to be focused yet flexible, single-minded yet adaptable, and that is one of the great gifts he has bequeathed to his followers in the Society of Jesus and beyond. The Jesuit stories that follow in this book offer a glimpse of how the vision of Ignatius has persisted through almost 500 years, expressed in all sorts of different ways in the changing circumstances of time and place, yet centred on the single goal of 'helping souls' in intimate companionship with Jesus.

Part 2
Sent on Mission

They should keep before their eyes the greater
service of God and the universal good.
(Constitutions 622)

~ 2 ~

Pierre Favre (1506–46)

Patrick Carberry SJ

[What impresses me about Favre] is his dialogue with all, even the most remote, and even with his opponents; his simple piety, a certain naïveté perhaps, his being available straightaway, his careful interior discernment, the fact that he was a man capable of great and strong decisions but also capable of being so gentle and loving.

– Pope Francis

If you stand outside the austere Collège Sainte-Barbe in rue Valette in Paris, you can easily imagine the noisy students coming and going there in the early sixteenth century. University life then, as today, was full of the energy and enthusiasm of youth; but it could also be tough. Step back in time for a moment and glance inside the building. You will probably be struck by the spartan conditions the students have to endure: dark corridors, bare boards, meagre diet and strict discipline. Open the heavy door and wander around for a while; you may chance upon a room with three beds, three desks, three chairs; a room shared by three young students. The year is 1529.

On closer inspection, you notice that one of the students is not so young. Ignatius, from Loyola in the north of Spain, is in his late thirties and showing the effects of the punishing life he has been leading since he turned his back on his family's fortune seven years ago. Take a closer look and you will see that there is something about his presence – serenity, a sense of purpose – that marks him out as a natural leader. Next to him is another Spaniard, from Xavier, not too far from Loyola. Francis, twenty-three years old, is full of the joys of youth: athletic, ambitious and popular amongst the students. He is anxious to restore the wealth and prestige that his family has lost in a recent defeat in war. He keeps his distance from Ignatius, wary of his dreams.

A Sensitive Soul

The third student, Pierre Favre, is the same age as Francis, but from a wholly different background. Brought up in Savoy, high in the French Alps, he has inherited the humble ways of his people. He is, like them, a shepherd at heart, but he also possesses a bright and inquisitive mind. Uniquely among his family and neighbours, as a young boy he was offered the chance of free education in a nearby school, and his outstanding success there has opened the door for him to Paris and to the prestigious university of the Sorbonne – and to Ignatius.

The two men, despite the difference in their age and backgrounds, quickly form a bond. Pierre helps Ignatius with his study of Aristotle, while Ignatius helps Pierre on his journey to God. Pierre is already a deeply religious man, imbued with the simple faith of his people. He is also a sensitive soul, and is prone to bouts of self-doubt, anxiety and scrupulosity. With patient perseverance, Ignatius helps his younger roommate to explore the inner world of his heart, to understand his struggles and face his fears, and to discover a compassionate God who has great plans for our world. As Ignatius guides him through the prolonged experience of the Spiritual Exercises, Pierre arrives at a place of deeper trust and more lasting peace. Above all, he finds in himself a desire to play his part in God's great enterprise in the world. Later in life, Ignatius would claim that Favre was the most gifted of all his early companions in leading others through the Spiritual Exercises, and that gift he would use to the full.

Open to Everyone

Pierre's sensitive nature gave him a profound sympathy with other people in their struggles and anxieties. That sensitivity, together with his unshakable trust in God and his innate gentleness, made him instantly approachable, even lovable, to all sorts of people. Whatever their background, whatever their story, everyone felt accepted by Pierre. He did not have the formidable presence of Ignatius, or the electric energy of Francis Xavier; his qualities were of a quieter, more intimate kind. 'Take care never to close your heart to anyone', he once advised, and that advice he put into practice in a remarkable way – and in remarkable times.

By the time they arrived in Rome in 1539, the little group of three had expanded to ten. They had all been ordained – Pierre was the first priest among them – and their reputation had gone abroad as 'the reformed priests', although their preferred name for themselves was 'the Company of Jesus'. It was under this name that they won the approval of the Pope for a new and innovative religious order – an order that broke with many of the received conventions of religious life and that was to be notable above all for its mobility.

Not being tied to a particular place or monastery, the Jesuits liked to think of the whole world as their cloister. Their spirit is reflected most dramatically in the amazing travels of Francis Xavier to 'the Indies': travels that took him to India, Indonesia, Japan and eventually to the fringe of China itself. Pierre's short life as a Jesuit was less dramatic. It was confined to Europe, but a Europe that was quickly becoming almost as alien as the new territories Xavier was discovering in the east. Religious unrest and political turmoil were stirring throughout the old world, and Pierre's travels brought him face-to-face with a severely demoralised Catholic Church and a rapidly expanding alternative version of Christianity. He was deeply disturbed by what he saw.

Pastoral Outreach

Pierre's first assignment, in 1539, was to Parma in the north of Italy, a city bitterly divided by rival factions and violent disputes. Accompanied by another Jesuit, Diego Laínez, Pierre quickly made his presence felt, not by addressing the social unrest directly, but by appealing in his sermons to deeper values, by his patience and gentleness in the confessional and, above all, by the depth of his conversations as he gave the Spiritual Exercises to an ever-increasing number of people. Under his inspiration, a quiet revolution was taking place in Parma, one that began with an inner conversion of the heart and was leading towards a transformation of society. This was the approach Pierre employed in his ministry for the rest of his life.

As word spread of Pierre's impact in Parma, requests began to arrive from religious and secular rulers for his presence elsewhere, and the remaining six years of his life were spent in response to their frequent demands. During those years he is estimated to have travelled some 20,000 km, on foot or by mule, moving mostly between Spain and Portugal in the south and Germany in the north. During the two periods he spent in the Iberian Peninsula (1541–42 and 1544–46) he developed further the pastoral strategy he had employed in Parma. In order to strengthen the faltering faith he found among both clergy and laity, he set about engaging with them in a personal way by means of 'confessions, conversations and the Exercises'. Confession for him was not merely a mechanical exercise, but an opportunity to initiate a personal conversation with each individual penitent. Such conversations frequently led to more prolonged spiritual direction, resulting in many cases in some form of the Spiritual Exercises, adapted to the circumstances of each person.

Fears for Germany

Pierre's first visit to Germany (1540–41) shocked him to the core. If mediocrity characterised the Church in much of Europe, in Germany it appeared to be in the process of disintegration. Sent by Pope Paul III to assist in the discussions between Catholics and Protestants in the city of Worms, Pierre quickly realised that heated arguments were not only ineffective, but were making matters worse. By the time the discussions moved to Ratisbon, it was clear that the talks were doomed to acrimonious failure. Pierre, who had little time for abstract debates and sterile controversy anyway, was more convinced than ever that a different approach was needed, one that addressed not so much the perceived errors of the Reformers as the failings of Catholics themselves. And so he spent his time preaching and giving lectures, and particularly in hearing confessions, meeting individuals for spiritual direction and giving the Spiritual Exercises.

After spending some months in Spain, Pierre was summoned once again to Germany in 1542, this time to help with the preparation of the Church's response to the accelerating crisis there. By the time he arrived, however, initial plans for the reform of Catholic life were already well advanced, and Pierre found himself available to respond to requests for his presence, first in Speyer, then in Mainz and later in Cologne. By this time, as he says himself, he had developed a deep affection for the German people, even though he had to struggle 'against despair of any good for Germany'. A year later, when word got around that he had been summoned to Portugal, there was uproar in Cologne, and a petition was signed by the citizens of that city demanding that he be allowed to stay – but it was not to be. He left Germany for the last time in August 1544.

Sentiments of Love and Hope

Pierre's radical approach to the crisis of his age is nowhere more evident than in his attitude towards the Lutherans. At a time of growing bitterness and division between Catholics and Protestants, often accompanied by vitriolic language and slanderous gossip, Pierre not only refrained from harsh judgements, but he positively rejoiced at the 'sentiments of love and hope God gave me … towards all heretics', as he notes in his diary. Such an attitude, he believed, must be the starting point for any fruitful dialogue. In a letter to a fellow Jesuit, who had asked for Pierre's advice about how to deal with the

Lutherans, he wrote that 'we must be careful to regard them with love, to love them in deed and in truth, and to banish from our own souls any thought that might lessen our love and esteem for them. This can be done by speaking familiarly with them about subjects on which we agree and by avoiding points of discussion that may give rise to argument; for argument usually ends in one side lording it over the other. We must first seek to establish concord by dwelling on what unites us.'

'We must establish concord by dwelling on what unites us': that was the constant vision that inspired Pierre in those troubled times. He knew in the depths of his heart that what ultimately unites us can be found not in clever arguments, or structural reforms or doctrinal formulations, but by humbly acknowledging our limitations and placing our trust in the one who enables us to rise above them. This was the lesson he had first learned from Ignatius in that dingy room in rue Valette many years before. This was the source of the hope he brought to struggling Catholics in strife-torn Europe. This was the meaning of the extraordinary prayer that Pierre valued so much and resolved to make frequently: a prayer for 'the Pope, the Emperor, the King of France, the King of England, Luther, the Grand Turk, Bucer and Philip Melanchthon'. In that prayer Pierre was able to gather them all together – Catholics, Protestants and Muslims – in the presence of the compassionate gaze of the Father.

In early spring 1546 Pierre received a summons from the Pope to leave Portugal and go to Trento in the north of Italy as an official theologian at the council that had just begun. He never made it. At this stage, Pierre's health, which was never robust, was deteriorating quickly, no doubt exacerbated by his constant travels and labours. In mid-July, a mere seven years since his first mission to Parma, Pierre Favre arrived back in Rome to be with Ignatius one last time. He died in the presence of his old friend and spiritual guide on 1 August 1546. He was forty years of age.

He was canonised by Pope Francis on 17 December 2013.

~ 3 ~

Claude la Colombière (1641–82)

David Stewart SJ

> God is in the midst of us, or rather we are in the
> midst of God; wherever we are, God sees us and
> touches us: at prayer, at work, at table and at
> recreation.
>
> – Claude la Colombière

There are more illustrious Jesuit saints than Claude la Colombière, the gentle Frenchman who was the spiritual director of St Margaret Mary Alacoque, but Claude's legacy is as valuable as any of theirs. Like Margaret Mary, Claude is forever associated with devotion to the Sacred Heart. What is less well known is that for several years he lived and ministered in London; indeed, at the Court of St James in Westminster. The suffering he endured there, in the anti-Catholic atmosphere of the time, was so awful that it almost certainly contributed to his early death. Through no fault of his own, this gentle apostle of the heart of Christ got horribly caught up in the political intrigues of the time, when his sole desire was to bring consolation into the frequently burdensome lives of people. The emphasis on God's love and mercy, which is at the centre of all devotion to Christ's heart, remained the foundation of everything Claude did in his priestly ministry during his short earthly life.

Early Years

Claude was born to a well-to-do family in 1641 in Saint-Symphorien-d'Ozon, close to Lyons in south-east France. Growing up in a caring and supportive family, he had good friends and developed a great love for literature and the arts. His primary education took place in the small city of Vienne, a short distance away, where his family had settled. Claude was enrolled for his secondary education at the Jesuit college in Lyons, an institution that was to play a significant part in his future life. During his school years, he began to feel a call to the priesthood in the Society of Jesus and, on reaching the age of seventeen, he entered the novitiate, which was located in those days in Avignon.

His early years in the Jesuits were not easy. Claude had a vivid sense of his own unworthiness, and he experienced at times a terrible aversion to life in the novitiate. Nevertheless, he persevered and pronounced his first vows after the usual two years. He then remained in Avignon for his initial studies. Regency – a period of direct apostolic work and a distinctive feature of Jesuit formation – was also spent in Avignon, where for five years he taught grammar and literature in the Jesuit College. After this, his superiors sent him to Paris to study theology. Ordained priest in 1669, he returned to Lyons to serve in the Jesuit college and church. During his time there, his reputation as a gentle preacher and a sensitive guide in spiritual direction spread rapidly throughout the region.

A Decisive Time

Claude made his Tertianship in Lyons in 1674. Tertianship is the final year of Jesuit formation, known as 'the school of the heart', during which the Spiritual Exercises of St Ignatius are made for the second time, over a period of thirty days. This was a decisive year for Claude, a time of prayerful discernment during which God was preparing him for what was to come. There is a key phase in the Spiritual Exercises during which Ignatius encourages the retreatant to make a 'choice of a way or state of life'. As he reflected on his calling, Claude had a strong sense that he needed to deepen his personal sanctity and to become more open to those he encountered in his ministry. To that end, and in order to be a truly effective apostle, he took the unusual step of making a private vow, in addition to the public vows he professed as a Jesuit, to observe the Constitutions of the Society with utmost fidelity.

His Tertianship finished, Claude was sent to be the superior of a small community in Paray-le-Monial in the Burgundy region. This must have surprised some of his fellow Jesuits. They must have wondered why this energetic and engaging preacher was being sent to a small, obscure town, far from any of the great centres of population and the magnificent churches to be found in them. Yet it was here that Claude's most powerful mission began to unfold, a mission that would have a huge influence on the whole Catholic world. For it was here that he met Margaret Mary Alacoque.

Faithful Servant, Perfect Friend

Near to the Jesuit church in that small and pretty town, there was – and still is – a convent of the Visitation Sisters. Margaret Mary was a member of that community. She had recently been undergoing some strange and unsettling spiritual experiences. In a world where a harsh version of the Christian message, known as Jansenism, was being promoted, she felt that Jesus had been revealing his heart to her, giving her a glimpse of his great compassion for the world, and calling her to make that known. Even though these visions brought her consolation and were clearly intended for the consolation of others, her community and her superior had concluded that she was delusional. Margaret Mary was distressed and confused by their reaction. Still, in the midst of all the pain, she believed that the Lord was promising to send her a 'faithful servant and perfect friend', someone who would both understand and guide her.

In February 1675 that friend arrived, the skilled and kind spiritual companion, Fr Claude. Like any good spiritual director, he listened more than he spoke. Together, in the characteristically Ignatian ministry of spiritual conversation, they explored the inspirations that Margaret Mary had been receiving concerning devotion to Christ's heart. Over time, they discerned the presence of the Holy Spirit in what she had experienced. Convinced of the genuineness of the revelations, Claude gave her the reassurance that others, including her superior, had been unable to do. He encouraged Margaret Mary to trust her experience.

Devotion to the Sacred Heart

These days, some people find the image of the Sacred Heart somewhat tired and over-familiar. Others find themselves ill at ease with the traditional representations of the devotion, for these are not always attractive to today's sensibilities. There can also be a more general temptation among certain people today to mock popular devotions. Yet, if approached with an open mind and generosity of spirit, devotion to the Sacred Heart can reveal surprising depths.

Devotion to the Sacred Heart is Ignatian in many ways, as Claude would have quickly seen. Ignatius, through the graces given to him, could see into the heart of things. He spoke of 'finding God in all things' as a grace given to him but offered to everyone. His was a mysticism of everyday life, as one writer has put it. Ignatius also had a deep devotion to the Trinity. His is a mysticism of the Trinity, an experience of being drawn into the inner life of God in all its mystery and differentiated unity. His mysticism is also thoroughly Christ-centred. In the pierced heart of Jesus upon on the Cross, he saw the inexhaustible love of God shared with all people. Although Ignatius never mentions the Sacred Heart – the language was not used in his time – clearly he felt himself privileged by an insight into the inner being of God, made manifest to the whole world on the cross, and present in the whole of created reality.

A Difficult Assignment

Claude's assignment to Paray-le-Monial proved to be brief. Jesuits everywhere attempt to hold themselves in readiness to respond to new opportunities and to be sent to new frontiers, even when their current work appears successful. Jesuits are meant to be men on the move. Barely a year and a half after his arrival in Paray-le-Monial,

Claude found himself on his way to England where, more than a century after the Reformation, there was still much hostility towards Catholics. Claude was sent on a delicate mission: to be chaplain to the Duke and Duchess of York. The duke, a Catholic convert, was the younger brother and heir-presumptive of the reigning king, Charles II; the duchess, Mary Beatrice, or Mary of Modena, was a devout Catholic from birth. King Charles had granted the couple special permission to maintain a chapel in St James's Palace. The English Jesuits were still in considerable disarray in those days, and so a request came to the French Jesuits for a suitable chaplain. Claude was given a modest apartment in the palace and moved in on 13 October 1676.

The new chaplain found it difficult from the beginning. By all accounts, that first London winter was severe; perhaps imprudently, Claude refused any extra heating for himself in his sparse apartment. He also admitted to finding London cuisine inedible. But physical hardships were not his main concerns. The morals of the Restoration era were lax and louche, as contemporary literary evidence shows. Claude was distressed by what he saw but, despite that, he refused to harangue the people; instead, he returned again and again in his preaching to the love of Christ's heart. As one biographer puts it, 'he breathed goodwill'. Claude's spiritual diary of that time records an increasing devotion to St Francis de Sales (1567–1622), the gentle bishop of Geneva, and it's easy to see why this saint appealed to him. In Claude's preaching we find a similar emphasis on the tenderness of God, his unlimited mercy and love and, in contrast, the boundless ingratitude that people show in return. All of this also echoes, of course, those spiritual conversations that Claude had undertaken with Margaret Mary in Paray-le-Monial.

Serious trouble lay ahead, however. Seventeenth-century London was an uneasy place for Catholics, and especially for Jesuits. In one of the strangest episodes of British history in the post-Reformation period, an entirely fictitious conspiracy, dreamt up by one Titus Oates, gripped the kingdom between 1678–81. Catholics, it alleged, were plotting against the life of Charles II, and the Jesuits were the ringleaders. A decade earlier, hysterical rumours had been circulating that the Great Fire of London had been the work of the Jesuits. Now, fresh rumours began to circulate, claiming that the Jesuits in England were planning the 'Popish Plot'. Oates claimed to have attended a meeting in a tavern on The Strand where the Jesuits' tactics were discussed. Caught up in this wave of frenzy, Claude was denounced by someone whom he thought he could trust. Nine Jesuits, including the Provincial, were executed. Imprisoned in November 1678 in an unheated filthy dungeon, his health, which had never been strong, rapidly deteriorated. Charged with making traitorous statements against the king and parliament, Claude was lucky to escape death himself. Instead, he was deported back to France in 1679, a seriously ill man. Upon his return, his health continued to deteriorate. He eventually made his way back to Paray-le-Monial where, after one final meeting with Margaret Mary, he died on 15 February 1682, at the age of forty-one.

Source of Consolation
Devotion to the Sacred Heart did not begin with Margaret Mary and Claude la Columbière, of course. Its origins can be traced back through the Middle Ages to the New Testament itself. However, the modern devotion, as it has come down to us, can be traced especially to Paray-le-Monial in the seventeenth century, at a time when a harsh and merciless version of the gospel was being promoted by the Jansenists. It is largely through the example and inspiration of Claude la Colombière that the devotion was entrusted in a special way to the Jesuits. From small beginnings, the devotion spread throughout France and beyond, until it became a powerful source of consolation for Catholics worldwide. Over the years, it has taken on many forms, including the international prayer movement, the Apostleship of Prayer, now known as the Pope's Worldwide Prayer Network.

In 1856, Pope Pius IX instituted the Feast of the Sacred Heart as a major celebration in the universal Church. Claude la Colombière was canonised by Pope John Paul II in 1992.

~ 4 ~

Rupert Mayer (1876–1945)

Peter Knox SJ

> In these last weeks in solitude I believe I have come
> into far closer contact with God Almighty in my
> own self ... I feel not the very least worry or anxiety
> about my future. I place all that in God's good hands.
> In myself I am completely contented and at peace.
>
> – Rupert Mayer

The first time I visited my grandparents in Bavaria, my grandfather, then in his eighties, took me to Munich to see the sights. After the mandatory stops in the cathedral and the neighbouring Jesuit parish of St Michael's, we went into the basement of the town hall, where I came across an unusual sight. Streams of people, laden with shopping bags, were quietly going in and out. They clearly weren't coming to pay their electricity bills, because there was a reverential silence about the place, which was gently lit with candles. They were coming to pray at the tomb of Rupert Mayer, Munich's twentieth-century saint. Due to the number of people coming to venerate him, Rupert's remains had been transferred from the Jesuit cemetery, in the suburb of Pullach, to the city centre. Now, many years after his death, Rupert Mayer was still drawing a daily crowd in the thousands. The only other place I have seen such posthumous veneration is at the tomb of St John Paul II in the crypt of St Peter's

Basilica in Rome. It was Pope John Paul who declared Rupert Mayer blessed in 1987.

After spending some time at the tomb, we went out into the busy city centre. My grandfather then told me something of the life of Rupert Mayer, a prominent figure during his youth in the city. In the fashionable streets of Bavaria's capital, it was difficult to imagine the same city populated with indigent people needing a full-time chaplain. However, in those days, between the Hauptbahnhof and Marienplatz, queues of people would wait for hours outside St Michael's Church to speak to Fr Mayer. This was during the time of the Weimar Republic, when the German economy had collapsed following the Treaty of Versailles, which compelled Germany to repay millions of US dollars that it could ill afford. In 1923, hyper-inflation was the order of the day and then, in 1929, came the Wall Street Crash. Impoverished citizens of Bavaria came flocking to Munich looking for a means to survive.

Having been appointed to work with these refugees, Rupert personally collected and distributed food and clothing, and found jobs and accommodation for the homeless and desperate. As he served Christ in the poor of his day, he was not naïve about the possibility of being duped. He said on one occasion that he would rather be deceived into helping nine people who didn't really require help than risk turning away a tenth person who was in real desperate need.

Even today, behind the prosperous façade of boutiques and pavement cafés, Munich – like most cities – still has a less well-to-do underbelly. The homeless and the substance-dependent still hang around the Hauptbahnhof waiting for a meal or a fix. *Fleiss* – hard work – is not enough to guarantee prosperity in tough economic times. To this day, charitable societies founded by Rupert Mayer or named after him still serve the poor and those in need in Munich.

Rupert was born in Stuttgart in 1876 to a family of six children. He trained initially as a diocesan priest and was ordained at the age of twenty-three; the following year he joined the Jesuits. After completing six years of further Jesuit training, he criss-crossed the Netherlands, Switzerland and Germany giving retreats to laypeople. In 1912 he began his life's work with the poor of Munich. Apart from a period spent as a volunteer military chaplain in the First World War, and extended periods of incarceration for his outspoken opposition to Nazi ideologies, his apostolate to the poor continued until his death in 1945.

As chaplain to Bavarian forces during the First World War, Rupert turned down the offer of working in a field hospital, opting instead to be a consoling presence to soldiers on the front lines. In the trenches of the battlefields in France, Romania and Poland, Rupert inspired and consoled the men to whom he ministered – Catholic and Protestant alike. He was known for his bravery under terrifying conditions, and for risking his own life while rescuing injured men from the line of fire. His major tasks as chaplain were to celebrate the sacraments – particularly the Eucharist and Reconciliation – to care for the dying and then to bury the countless soldiers killed in battle. For his exemplary valour, he was awarded the Iron Cross, 2nd Class, in March 1915, the first time this honour was bestowed on a chaplain.

In 1916, in Romania, Rupert's left leg was shredded by shrapnel from a grenade, and had to be amputated. Using a prosthesis, Rupert limped for the rest of his life, not unlike St Ignatius Loyola, the founder of the Society of Jesus, who in the siege of Pamplona in 1521 had his leg shattered by a cannon ball. The leg, which was to cause Rupert great suffering in subsequent years, earned him the nickname, 'the limping priest'.

Returning to Munich after the First World War, Rupert resumed his ministry of caring for the poor of the city. People who came to him found in him an understanding priest. He dispensed not only food and clothing, but also realistic spiritual advice. He was a renowned preacher, and was particularly in demand in the confessional. Inspired perhaps by his namesake, St Rupert, the seventh-century apostle of Bavaria who founded monasteries in the area, Rupert Mayer built up associations of laypeople to bring Christian compassion to Munich, with much success. For example, during his time as the chaplain to the men's Congregation of Mary, its membership doubled to over 7,000.

In the period between the wars, Rupert not only served the poor of the city, but extended his ministry to whoever needed it. My grandfather, at the time a young man in Munich, told me how he would sometimes encounter Fr Mayer on Sundays, celebrating Mass at the main train station as early as 3 a.m. He was there so that people who could afford a day out in the countryside would be able to fulfil their Sunday obligation before the departure of the first train.

Perhaps it was his experience of so much carnage and pointless death in the trenches of the First World War that gave Rupert a loathing for any ideology of hate. With equal vehemence, he denounced the programmes of communism and national socialism, to which Germans in the 1920s and 1930s were turning in ever greater numbers. The Weimar state was weak, and extremist voices like Hitler's gave promise of a resurgent, prouder Germany. It took a strong character to speak out against such populist ideology. Rupert's forthright denunciation of the Nazis' attempts to close Church schools provoked the government of the day into banning him from preaching. Undaunted, he continued to do so, and in 1937 he received a six-month suspended prison sentence. He still continued to preach, however, until he was silenced by Church authorities anxious not to incur the wrath of the state. But that soon changed. After the Prefect of Munich made a particularly defamatory statement, Rupert's superiors allowed him to preach again in public. For this, he was promptly arrested and imprisoned in Landsberg Prison – the same prison where Adolf Hitler had been imprisoned after his abortive 1924 Beer Hall *Putsch*, and where, after the Second World War, hundreds of condemned war criminals were executed. Five months later, upon his release from Landsberg in a general amnesty, Rupert resumed his preaching of the Christian message, fearlessly denouncing Nazi ideology at every opportunity.

Seen as a threat to the regime, Rupert was incarcerated in 1940 in the Sachsenhausen concentration camp outside Berlin. During my visit to Munich, my grandfather took me to visit Dachau, and I subsequently went to Sachsenhausen to see for myself where Rupert had been held captive. I marvelled at how harsh, heartless and efficient these camps were, built in pursuit of a deranged racist ideology. As half-Jews, my relatives were held in some of these camps and forced to work in munitions factories. My grandfather's brother, Franz, an art dealer, was imprisoned during the war for helping Jewish people to sell their treasures. Unlike millions of others, they were among the lucky ones who managed to escape with their lives.

While in Sachsenhausen, Rupert's health declined steadily. The Nazis, fearing that they might have a high-profile martyr on their hands, transferred him after some months to the Benedictine Abbey in Ettal, in the foothills of the Bavarian Alps, where he was placed under house arrest. It so happened that another heroic figure of the time, the Lutheran pastor Dietrich Bonhoeffer, also stayed at the abbey during the winter of 1940, where he was sheltered by the monks. He, however, was less fortunate than Rupert Mayer and was executed in Flossenbürg concentration camp just twenty-three days before the German surrender in April 1945. Rupert remained in Ettal from August 1940 until his release in May 1945, when he returned to a devastated Munich.

During his various incarcerations, Rupert was particularly concerned that his silence might be misconstrued as capitulation to the Nazi demands that he cease preaching against the state. He wanted it to be clear that blaming Jews, communists, homosexuals, foreigners, intellectuals, church people, conscientious objectors, artists or any other group of people for Germany's woes, and victimising them in consequence, was totally unacceptable to the Christian vision. His uncompromising rejection of this Nazi ideology made the sometimes mealy-mouthed official Church seem timid by comparison. Growing up, as I did, in South Africa during the apartheid regime, I am conscious of the power of prophetic voices, and I look back in gratitude to people like Archbishops Desmond Tutu and Denis Hurley OMI, who suffered persecution for their outspoken condemnation of hateful ideology. We must surely be grateful whenever such fearless voices are raised in times of crisis.

During his years in Ettal, it pained Rupert that he was isolated from his beloved people and unable to minister to his suffering compatriots. The beauty of the countryside surrounding the abbey in Ettal was no compensation for his desire to care for the urban poor of war-torn Bavaria. Freed from house arrest by American forces in May 1945, he returned to St Michael's at once, where he received a hero's welcome. However, his health had been undermined by stress and imprisonment, and he died of a stroke six months later, on 1 November, while celebrating Mass.

These days, as I teach Jesuit scholastics in Nairobi about the Second Vatican Council, two things strike me in particular about Rupert Mayer. First, throughout his life, he anticipated this greatest of Church councils by promoting the apostolate of the laity. Rupert was unable to take care by himself of all of the poor who came to him. And so, he set about helping lay people to develop their spiritual life, attending not only to their growth in prayer, but directing it into active concern for the poor. This notion was taken up by the fathers of the Second Vatican Council in their Decree on the Apostolate of the Laity. Secondly, Rupert's ministry to soldiers, of whatever denomination or none, was a feature of his time as a military chaplain. Such inclusive service was later a motivating force for the ecumenical movement. If one could pray in the trenches with Christians of other persuasions, why should the church not do likewise in peacetime? This insight eventually paved the way for the Decree on Ecumenism at the Second Vatican Council.

I frequently ask myself what we can learn now from Rupert Mayer's steadfast and outspoken denunciation of Nazism and Communism. Today, over seventy years after his death, our own times are not completely different from his. Once again, populist politicians around the world are appealing to various sectors of the societies that they claim to represent. They offer a demoralised people the vision of a renewed nation, ready to be made 'great again'. As always, in reinventing the national story, a scapegoat must be found and some group held responsible for our woes. For Hitler, it was the Jews, communists, Romanies and homosexuals. For modern demagogues, it is immigrants who are to blame, who are portrayed as 'stealing our jobs'. In the rhetoric of the demagogue, all problems will be solved by dealing with these 'parasites on our system'. Build walls and expel the vulnerable is their message, and local people will become prosperous once again. The golden age will be once more.

Rupert Mayer saw through this unsubtle manipulation of popular nationalist sentiment and, at considerable cost to himself, denounced it for the injustice it inflicted on the victims of prejudice. Are we doing enough today to ensure that similar injustices do not take root once again in our society?

~ 5 ~

Pierre Teilhard de Chardin (1881-1955)

David John Ayotte SJ

> The time has come to realise that an interpretation
> of the universe – even a positivist one – remains
> unsatisfying unless it covers the interior as well as
> the exterior of things; mind as well as matter. The
> true physics is that which will, one day, achieve the
> inclusion of man in his wholeness in a coherent
> picture of the world.
>
> – Pierre Teilhard de Chardin

When one recalls the shapers of Christian thought beyond the biblical tradition, figures such as Augustine in the fourth century and Thomas Aquinas in the Middle Ages quickly come to mind. Most people struggle, however, to name a similar figure for our own era, with its shift from a stable unchanging worldview to one that embraces evolution, developmental psychology and Einstein's theory of relativity. With time, I suspect that Pierre Teilhard de Chardin may well be the one who best describes theologically our age and its rapid pace of change.

Years of Formation
Born in the Auvergne region of France in 1881, Teilhard was the fourth of eleven children. From the age of twelve, he was educated

by the Jesuits in their boarding school near Lyons, and on completion of his secondary education in 1899 he decided to join the Jesuits. During the normal course of studies, he showed an aptitude for theological thinking, while simultaneously developing his great love for palaeontology, the study of the origins of life.

In 1901, because of the *lois d'exception* enacted in the early years of the twentieth century, it was very difficult for religious to work or study in France. So, as a type of exile, Teilhard and his classmates lived and studied on the British Channel Islands off the coast of Normandy. He later completed his theological studies in Hastings on the mainland of Great Britain. In Jersey, where he lived among some of the finest scholars of France, Teilhard explored some of the current creative thinking of modern science as it related to the Catholic tradition and the philosophical classics. It was his creative fusion of the physical sciences and theological studies that prompted Teilhard, in the light of the findings of the fossils of Neanderthal man, to explore in a new way such traditional notions as original sin.

Thinking of this kind was unacceptable in the context of the Church of that time, however, and prompted his superiors to forbid him to publish anything further in the area of theology. It was only after his death that his theological work was taken up by those who saw it as pivotal in bringing theology into dialogue with contemporary science. Indeed, many of these same thinkers would go on to shape the thought of the Second Vatican Council. Since then, Teilhard's exploratory theological works have been affirmed by such important figures as Pope Benedict XVI in 2009 and by Pope Francis in his major encyclical of 2015, *Laudato Si'*.

Problems with Authority

Of particular significance in the development of Teilhard's thought was the Great War (1914–18) when, as a young priest, he was called away from his palaeontological research to become a stretcher-bearer and chaplain to a Moroccan regiment of light infantry. It was his experience during the war that would shape his perspective on the evolution of human consciousness. There in the trenches, in the midst of bitter hostilities, a vision of unity emerged for him which melded theology, science and personal loss. Eventually, Teilhard would receive the highest honour France had to offer, the *légion d'honneur*, for his work in the trenches. A still greater fruit emerged from his experience in Verdun and Yser, however: the notion of the 'noosphere', a global mind of humanity.

Following the war, and having studied among some of the leading thinkers in the field of palaeontology, Teilhard was invited on a temporary basis to assist Émile Licent, founder of the Museum of Natural History outside of Beijing. It was there that the course of Teilhard's life was radically altered. A draft of his thinking on original sin, having reached the eyes of his superiors, caused such a stir that he was forbidden to publish any of his theological reflections for the rest of his life. Despite repeated efforts to have this censure lifted, Teilhard's theology never entered the public sphere in his day. While remaining faithful to the Church and obedient to his superiors' strictures, his closest friends remembered the repeated bouts of depression that would haunt him for the rest of his life.

What began as a simple invitation for a short period of research in China became an extended period of exile, lasting until 1946. While in China, under the leadership of his friend Davidson Black, Teilhard became closely involved with the discovery and interpretation of important fossils known as Peking Man. Following the end of the Second World War, and on his return to France, Teilhard's name became a cause célèbre, and he was elected to the prestigious Académie des Sciences in 1951. His superiors, however, nervous about his rapidly rising popularity, asked him to quickly leave family and friends in Paris to assume a less visible life in New York. There, in 1955, he passed away in the late afternoon of Easter Sunday, having tea with a few close friends.

Towards the Omega Point
Largely building on the vocabulary of phenomenology, with its concentration on consciousness, Teilhard developed a view of the universe in a state of growing awareness. All matter, from the atom

to the complex structures of the human mind, express various degrees of what he called 'complexity consciousness'. There is a process in creation, not only of external, physical evolution, but also of internal evolution – 'involution' – leading to the development of mind. In this model, the classic dualism of matter and mind is resolved. For Teilhard, there is a direction to evolution that does not negate freedom but enhances it. We are growing ever more free as we become more conscious of ourselves as individuals and as a community.

It can often be assumed that evolution has reached its peak in the individual human mind, but Teilhard would argue that the forces of evolution continue to take shape through the evolution and transformation of society, local and global, into a thinking whole. Whether we think of the early scripts recording the cultural memory of the Sumerians or the most advanced of today's technological innovations, humanity as a whole is becoming the thinking voice for all of creation. The *noosphere*, or collective mind, flows from the same physiological and biological forces of attraction that billions of years ago led to the formation of stars, planets and life.

While respecting the trial-and-failure process of evolution among all species, Teilhard held that there is a direction in creation that points towards the 'Omega Point'. This is the place of convergence of all truth and consciousness, awaiting its fulfillment by the Divine. This direction is understood in its earliest forms as gravity, while among life forms it appears as attraction. But with ever greater consciousness and self-reflection, we recognise it as the self-giving of love expressed and embodied in Jesus Christ. As the world becomes more and more 'Christic', we move out of our self-preoccupation to become people in service of the larger whole, the Body of Christ. Individuals find their identity and purpose in a reality greater than themselves. In Christian thought, especially in the epistles to the Colossians and Ephesians, we get a sense that this collective evolution is the same as the apostle Paul's experience of the Church as the Body of Christ, whose vocation is the transformation of humanity and creation.

A World becoming Eucharist

In Teilhard's thought, the Church is central as the concrete expression of the risen Christ, transforming the world now and in the future. It is also the place where creative ideas and inspirations regarding the goal and direction of humanity and creation are communicated. In a certain way, if humanity is the voice of all creation, the Church becomes the conscious voice of humanity's vocation of service. While humanity and creation are in need of further development, still the presence of Christ as head already shapes the rest of his communal body.

Such growth as a community is vitally linked to Teilhard's theology that the world and all creation are gradually becoming Eucharist. So often we view communion as something we receive rather than as something that God is doing to us through our cooperation. This latter view is more expressive of Teilhard's conviction that God is taking the whole universe and transforming it into his presence. Such a cosmology moved Pope Benedict XVI to state in 2009:

> The role of the priesthood is to consecrate the world so that it may become a living host, a liturgy: so that the liturgy may not be something alongside the reality of the world, but that the world itself shall become a living host, a liturgy. This is also the great vision of Teilhard de Chardin: in the end we shall achieve a true cosmic liturgy, where the cosmos becomes a living host.

Relevance for Today

Any cosmic theology, pointing to a future identity in Christ's body, must take account of the body of creation as it now exists: in formation, certainly, but also broken. Today, any imagining of the future requires that we incorporate into our thinking a respect for the environment. This is a call to assume responsibility for the future of coming generations. Teilhard was optimistic that, despite his extensive experience of war, humanity is moving forward. That said, the future we are moving towards cannot simply affirm human beings and their aspirations, but must take up a concern for the whole of creation. Humanity must be the voice of those creatures that have not been endowed with our reflective faculties and sense of responsibility. For this reason, many contemporary authors have rightly stated that Teilhard is today's needed theologian for the environment.

A mission for the environment must clearly embrace the planet and the socio-economic needs of the poorest. But Teilhard widens the vision beyond Earth itself. Mission, for Teilhard, reaches to the stars. He explores the notion of life on other planets, and the meaning of a Christ who comes not simply to save human beings, but every possible thinking species in the universe. It requires a major reshaping of theology to speak of how grace and sin touch not only our own species, but all creation to the ends of the universe. God is a God across galaxies, bringing completion, reconciliation and joy.

Given the ongoing explorations and discoveries of our times, the possibility of finding other life forms and other thinking species becomes ever more plausible. What would the gospel of the God-man mean for those who are not human? Teilhard begins the marvelous new journey of speculation, and offers conjectures that still must be developed, nuanced and corrected. His thought is a wonderful opening of our minds to a universe being 'Christified'. His theology unites what is happening here on earth to the unfolding mystery of an entire universe being 'divinised'.

For ourselves, when we are overwhelmed by the bitter calamities we encounter in our world today, this long-term perspective is really vital for us. We can so easily lose sight of the larger picture that the communal mind of God is painting with our lives. But time will tell where wisdom lies. My bet is that, when theologians come together in the not-too-distant future, they will speak of this humble man, who dug the soils of France and China and foresaw a world becoming Christ, as the doctor of the twentieth century who shaped the future of our thought.

~ 6 ~

Karl Rahner (1904–84)

James Corkery SJ

> What Christian faith teaches is never communicated
> merely by a conceptual indoctrination from without,
> but is, and can basically be experienced through, the
> supernatural grace of God as a reality in us.
>
> – Karl Rahner

The most memorable thing about this twentieth-century German Jesuit is his profound sense of the presence of God – and of how God can be *experienced* – in the midst of everyday life. He joined the Society of Jesus in 1922 at the age of eighteen, following in the footsteps of his older brother, Hugo. Afterwards, he spent his whole life as a Jesuit trying to communicate that which St Ignatius Loyola, the founder of the Jesuits, was also convinced of: that God could truly be experienced; indeed that God could be found in all things.

It was Karl Rahner's deepest desire to draw people into an awareness of how God was in no sense remote from them, distant and unconcerned, but rather at the heart of their lives, close to them in everything, bearing them up as they carried the burden of everyday existence with its toils, difficulties and disappointments. Rahner was able to find God in these latter particularly and, with the heart of a pastor, he did all he could to make God's presence visible for people in their daily drudgery, in the ups and downs of lives that were often full of love but also full of suffering.

Early Years

Karl Rahner himself came from a family of seven children. He was born in Freiburg, Germany, on 5 March 1904. His family was neither rich nor poor. His father was a schoolteacher who ended up as a professor at the teachers' college in the city. In order to provide well for the family, he took extra students for tutoring, and Karl's mother took care of additional children to add to the family income. The Rahner family, like most people in Freiburg at that time, was Catholic, although not excessively pious, and young Karl grew up in a Christian, Catholic atmosphere. He attended primary and secondary school in Freiburg, and said of himself that he had been an average student and had found his classes a bit boring.

On 20 April 1922, three weeks after leaving school, he entered the Jesuit novitiate in Feldkirch, Austria, and spent the next ten years – in Austria, Germany and Holland – preparing for priesthood in the Society of Jesus, mainly through the study of philosophy and theology. On 26 July 1932, he was ordained priest by Cardinal Michael Faulhaber at the Jesuit church of St Michael in Munich. After his ordination, his entire life was devoted to study, initially of philosophy, and subsequently – for five decades – of theology, until his death on 30 March 1984, at the age of eighty.

Theology, Prayer and Life

His life sounds boring, does it not? Studying and teaching theology, dealing with students, writing books and essays, carrying out ordinary academic tasks. But Rahner was not bored, nor was he boring, because everything he did was driven by his passion to communicate the nearness of God to ordinary people. The theological subject that engaged him most was grace. Grace is the word used to indicate God's closeness to human beings, God's gift of his own self to men and women, God's merciful, compassionate and loving presence in the lives and hearts of people.

Rahner was captivated by the Christian truth that the immense, mysterious, unimaginable God, who took his breath away, should take a personal interest in each human being and in the human world. He was in awe of this God who offers his abiding presence and love to everyone, calling all of us – not just Christians – to eternal life with him. Rahner loved this mysterious God, this warm mystery that underpins our lives. He was eager to know this holy mystery personally, to live in its embrace and to share with others how this loving presence lay at the heart of their lives.

Someone with a love like that at the centre of his life is neither bored nor boring! Rahner's teaching and writing is not just full of concepts; it is spiritually rich as well. Centred on God's generous gift of himself to all men and women, Rahner's theology is also a spirituality. It is about Christian life as lived as well as about thinking out Christian truths. Indeed, Rahner only wanted to think out these truths in order to be able to communicate them to others as realities in their lives. That's what the dry-sounding subject, theology, really is: a thinking-out of the Christian faith in ever-new contexts, seeking to make it intelligible to people in every situation of life.

When Rahner was engaged in some hard theological thinking, he was always simultaneously praying hard, and his prayer could be disarmingly simple. On one occasion, he told God that his infinity and greatness made him anxious and uneasy, and that he would like him to speak just a simple word that would reassure him and bring him peace. He asked for an 'abbreviated' word, adapted to his own smallness, something that he could grasp and that would enable him to breathe freely again. 'Don't tell me everything that you are,' he prayed, 'just say that you love me, just tell me of your goodness to me.' This was how Rahner always prayed. At the very end of his life, at a gathering to celebrate his eightieth birthday three weeks before he died, he asked those present to pray for him, 'to make perhaps just a small prayer in God's presence that his love and his mercy may finally be given me'. He longed for that love, he lived for that love, he communicated that love.

Pastoral Motivation

So Rahner, intellectual though he was, was simple at heart. He was always an ordinary priest too, someone who simply wanted to put people in contact with God. It was this motivation, not the desire to be a famous professor, that drove him. Something happened in his mid-thirties that contributed to his becoming so pastoral. He was sent to the University of Innsbruck, where the Jesuits had responsibility for the faculty of theology, but in 1938 the university was taken over by the Nazis and the Jesuits had to leave.

Rahner spent most of the war years in Vienna, teaching at the Pastoral Institute, and in the village of Mariakirchen in Lower Bavaria, doing pastoral work. These years of pastoral involvement were to prove very fruitful for him because, particularly in Vienna, he became aware of the gap that existed between several of the dogmas taught by the Church and the actual lives of men and women in the world. He saw that, while the Church was confident in its fixed, unchanging truths, people were living in a world in which nothing seemed fixed and unchanging. In a century of two world wars, wars that changed the map of the world and took the lives of many, what would the future bring? History seemed unmanageable and cruel. There was a growing awareness of constantly changing historical circumstances and how they had a huge effect on everything. How then could things of abiding significance, like God's becoming human in Jesus, happen in history?

The Church claimed that this event, although it occurred at a particular time, was permanent in its significance. Other teachings of the Christian faith were advanced with similar confidence. But people had increasing difficulty accepting the gap, which had now become an abyss, between their own historical awareness and the abiding truths of the Christian faith. Rahner saw this clearly, as he sought to communicate these truths. His passion for assuring people of the closeness and reliability of God led him to develop a way of thinking that was very sophisticated academically, yet pastorally effective. Through those who studied and communicated it, Rahner's thinking became highly influential on the lives of ordinary people struggling to believe in God, including those who were simply abandoning such a belief. Rahner grew and grew in significance as a Catholic theologian, not only in German-speaking lands but also in the wider world, not least through his influence on, and his official expert participation in, the Second Vatican Council (1962–65). Everyone who studied theology from the mid-1960s studied his works, which were translated into many languages. He had become the most widely read Catholic theologian of the twentieth century.

Starting from Below
Before Rahner, understanding theology started 'from above'. The teachings of the Church were clearly stated, defended against objections and, to some extent, set apart from the world's ways of thinking. Rahner, while committed to those teachings, had the genius to start in another place, 'from below'. His theology began from the experience of human beings. He focused in particular on what he called human 'transcendent experience'. This refers to how human beings have a kind of built-in openness to God that reveals itself in the central acts of the human person: acts of knowing, choosing and loving. Rahner was able to demonstrate that, in these finite human acts, the infinite is 'touched' or 'grasped' implicitly, in a way that is mostly unnoticed and unknowing, but true nonetheless.

Rahner taught that when we think out and state particular truths, choose particular values, or love particular persons, we do so against the unnoticed, but ever-present, background or horizon of infinite truth, infinite value and infinite love. We *imply* these as we engage with everyday truths, values and loves. Mostly we do not notice this, but we do it nonetheless as beings who are 'open at the top', oriented towards what is permanent and abiding, even as we engage with particular truths, values and loves. We possess, as we were created, a 'God-towardsness' (as Irish theologian, Tom Marsh, once called it). However, God has an 'us-towardsness', which is expressed supremely in his becoming human in Jesus.

So we are not alien to God and God is not alien to us. Our human make-up opens us out towards God, and his divine love causes him to spill into our reality. Thus, the gap between what is permanent and what is historical gets bridged: for historical human beings are revealed to have a structure that orients them to what is abiding and infinite; and the unchanging, infinite God is revealed to have a heart that orients him to what is finite, to us, to our history, into which he enters at a particular time and place.

A Further Call

Bringing the infinite and the finite together in this way, uncovering how human beings are like keyholes for the divine key, was an achievement of Karl Rahner that he gradually brought to bear on every area of Christian thought, in what eventually became over 4,000 publications during his lifetime. But the picture is still incomplete, and this has to do with what I mentioned already: our openness to the infinite. The reader will rightly see that this openness in itself would not be sufficient to enable us to become aware of this infinite as *God*, as the God of Christian faith, the God of love. God extended a further gift to us: an offer, made to absolutely everyone, of being able to encounter the infinite not only as a what, but also as a who.

This is where the centerpiece of Rahner's theology – God's offer of grace, of himself, to every person – plays its key role. For grace is strictly *supernatural*; it is God's universal self-offering *above and beyond* what is given with human transcendent experience. It is an offer of an intimate personal relationship, silent, mysterious and loving. It is an offer that beckons every human being towards God, towards a relationship with the One whose very name is Love. It is a call from the One at the heart of Rahner's prayer, the One he addressed so simply, 'Just say that you love me, just tell me of your goodness to me.' Rahner devoted his life's work to assuring us that we are not foolish to pray this prayer with trusting hearts. That is no small achievement for this remarkable, yet utterly ordinary, Jesuit.

~ 7 ~

Pedro Arrupe (1907–91)

Brian Grogan SJ

Nowadays, the world doesn't need words, but lives
which cannot be explained except through faith and
love for Christ's poor.

– Pedro Arrupe

Pedro Arrupe is becoming recognised as one of the towering figures
of twentieth century Catholic life. It is well said that when we can
see far ahead, it is because we stand on the shoulders of giants. Pedro
Arrupe, the twenty-eighth General of the Society of Jesus, was a
tiny man, as was St Ignatius, the founder of the Jesuits, but he had
the vision and soul of a giant. He has been referred to as the second
founder of the Jesuits; more profoundly he has been described as 'a
mystic with open eyes'.

Arrupe gazed on our messy world – the world of the atom bomb,
torture, poverty and clashes of ideologies – and saw it as God does.
He would say, 'See with the eyes of Christ, go wherever the need is
greatest, serve the faith and promote justice as best you can, and you
will find God!' When I met him in 1977 I asked him how he felt
things were moving along. His face lit up as he replied, 'On the one
hand everything is wonderful. On the other hand, all is not well!'
That response reveals the mystic with open eyes, neither lost in an
other-worldly spirituality nor cynical about the state of this world.

He believed that God is everywhere at work in the chaos of human affairs, and that God will bring everything to a glorious completion. Relying on God, he believed profoundly in prayer, and spent more than four hours each day in silent prayer.

Early Years

Born in 1907 in Bilbao, Northern Spain, Pedro Arrupe, like Ignatius, was a Basque. His family was a happy one; he had four sisters, older than himself. As a bright and idealistic student, he was captivated by the desire to heal people, so he studied medicine. A brilliant career was opening out for him when, in 1926, he went to Lourdes for three months as a member of the bureau which studies the authenticity of reported cures. There he verified two cures, and later recalled, 'I sensed God very close and tugging at me'.

In 1927 he joined the Jesuits, and asked to be sent to Japan, where Francis Xavier had laboured almost four centuries earlier, but he was told to wait. In 1932 the Jesuits were expelled from Spain by the government of the new republic. All Jesuit property was seized, and 2,700 Jesuits had to seek refuge elsewhere in Europe. This experience of injustice raised for Pedro issues about the relationship between faith and justice, the Church and the world – issues that shaped his perspectives for the remainder of his life.

Pedro found a home among the Belgian Jesuits, and in 1936 was ordained priest. He then went to the USA to complete his formation, and in 1938 was finally missioned to Japan. There he learned Japanese but, while he spoke six other languages, he was not a born linguist. Someone commented that he spoke Spanish in seven languages!

Turmoil in Japan

In December 1941, after the Japanese attack on Pearl Harbour and America's entry into the Second World War, he was arrested as an American spy, and spent thirty-three days in solitary confinement. There he contemplated the possibility of tortures such as many of his brethren had endured before him. He prayed for courage and found God close. 'It was beautiful,' he said, 'the solitude with Christ, a mystical experience, nothing in my cell, only me and Christ.' His eyes would fill with tears in telling this story. Again, he had here a direct experience of personal injustice. He began to ponder how the message of Christ could ever be heard above the din of hatred and violence.

Freed from prison, he was assigned in 1943 to be master of novices, where he prepared his starving charges to serve the spiritual needs of their people. And then tragedy struck. In the United States, the Manhattan Project – the creation of the atom bomb – was under way at immense cost. On the Feast of the Transfiguration, 6 August 1945, while homilies across the world carried a message of hope for the transfiguration of humanity, the A-bomb was dropped on the unsuspecting city of Hiroshima. It fell to earth with a blinding flash, a crashing thunder, a devastating blast and a deceptively beautiful mushroom cloud. It changed the history of humankind.

Pedro Arrupe, with his tiny band of novices, led the first rescue party into the flattened city in which 150,000 citizens had been annihilated. He brought over 200 scarred human survivors home to the Jesuit house. They had been burned, boiled, skinned, deafened, blinded and worse. He cared for them, using all the medical expertise he had learned years earlier. For him, the bomb was 'a mystery of iniquity, a permanent experience outside of history, engraved on my memory'. Again came the questions that would not go away: 'Where is God in all this? What is the role of the Church in the face of such horrors?'

A Visionary Leader
People got on with life as best they could, however, and in 1958 Pedro was appointed provincial of the Japanese province. Then, in 1965, as the Second Vatican Council was ending, he attended the thirty-first General Congregation of the Jesuits in Rome. A general congregation is the highest authority in the Society of Jesus, and consists of selected delegates from around the world. Pedro came as an outsider, hoping only to convince his brethren that they must

adapt radically to meet the needs of the contemporary world. His listeners must have been impressed, for they elected him as their new superior general. Then, for sixteen turbulent years, he spearheaded the renewal of the Jesuits and others for the service of the Church and the world, as requested by the Second Vatican Council.

Arrupe participated in the Synod of Bishops in 1971, the theme of which was 'Justice in the World'. Faithful to the mind of the synod, Arrupe's dream was to focus all Jesuit talents, resources and works on this single mission. He worked tirelessly with his fellow Jesuits for this, and in 1975 the thirty-second General Congregation approved a decree on 'The Service of Faith and the Promotion of Justice'. Its key insight was that there can be no preaching of the gospel without work for justice. Although this had been the theme of the synod of 1971, neither the Church nor the Society of Jesus was ready for it. Arrupe said later that the struggle to link faith and justice was one of the greatest challenges to the Society.

Times of Painful Tension

Arrupe was a charismatic leader and much loved by those who knew him and worked with him. His warm, sincere and unassuming manner, together with his enthusiasm and profound vision, communicated hope and energy to those he met. Yet, all was not well. Following the council, conflicts around aspects of renewal in the Church were rife in both the Church and the Society. Conservatives and liberals became highly polarised, with both sides pressing for the values they sincerely believed in. Opposition to Arrupe's vision, to his gentle use of authority, to his openness to experimentation, to his interpretation of the Ignatian charism, came especially from Spain, but also from bishops around the world. He became a sign of contradiction, and endured the painful tension between faithfulness to the inherited tradition and adjusting the Society to the contemporary world in line with the Second Vatican Council.

From 1975 to 1980 Arrupe laboured on, a figure of hope to many, a man full of creativity and inspiration. From his many travels throughout the world, he saw that of all the needy people, refugees were most at risk. Hence in 1980 he founded the Jesuit Refugee Service. Like Ignatius, he wanted his men to be ready 'to go where the need is greatest' and to identify with the unwanted of the earth. 'To incarnate the Ignatian vision,' he said, 'we must get ourselves out of the concrete!' He meant that Jesuits must be available, mobile and flexible.

Difficulties emerged between Arrupe and successive popes over his perceived failure to keep his men in order, especially in relation to the teaching authority of the Church. These difficulties caused Pedro much agony for, like Ignatius Loyola, his devotion to the figure of the Pope, and to the Church, was boundless. Though he tried hard, he was not a Vatican diplomat, and finally a clash of personalities and style with Pope John Paul II led him in 1980 to offer his resignation. But the Pope told him to stay on for the present, for the sake of the Church and the Society.

Years of Darkness
In 1981, Arrupe undertook an exhausting visit to the Philippines, in which he presided at fourteen eucharistic celebrations and gave twenty-six addresses. Wherever he went, he repeated the same challenge: to be available to serve people through faith and justice, but in a way that is 'rooted and grounded in love'. Arrupe then went on to Thailand, where he met some of the first Jesuits working with the Jesuit Refugee Service. To them he said:

> Please, be brave! I will tell you one thing. Don't forget it! Pray, pray much! The problems we have been discussing will not be resolved by human power. I am saying to you something that I want to underline, a message, perhaps my swansong for the Society. If we are at the forefront of a new apostolate, we must be illuminated by the Holy Spirit. We must have a basic union of minds for this new apostolate which is being born. Now we are going through the birth pangs! From this medical point of view I come to the end of my talk!

This dynamic swansong was delivered on the Feast of the Transfiguration, the thirty-sixth anniversary of the destruction of Hiroshima. That same day, on his flight home to Rome, he suffered a massive stroke, and his own world was blown apart.

There followed ten dark years spent in the Jesuit infirmary in Rome. Increasingly unable to communicate, he grew feeble and suffered much inner darkness. Despite his deep loyalty, he sensed that he had failed in his relationship with the Holy Father. Though almost mute, he could follow what was said to him. He felt marginalised, especially when in October 1981 the Pope appointed his own delegate, Fr Paolo Dezza SJ, rather than any of Arrupe's team, to prepare for the next General Congregation, which would accept his resignation and choose his successor. On that occasion, from a wheelchair and unable to speak himself, he had this, his final reflection, read to the gathered brethren:

> More than ever I find myself in the hands of God.
> This is what I have wanted all my life from my
> youth. But now there is a difference: the initiative is
> entirely with God. It is indeed a profound spiritual
> experience to know and feel myself so totally in
> God's hands.

His desolate decade came to a merciful end on 5 February 1991. He was eighty-three years old. Happily, the rift with Pope John Paul II was healed before he died.

A Challenging Legacy

Most of what Jesuits and their co-workers do is hidden, but it is sometimes written in blood. Arrupe knew that the struggle for faith and justice, carried out under the banner of the cross, would lead to conflict with dominant and powerful opponents. It is a stark reality that some ninety Jesuits from twenty countries have died violently on mission since the Society committed itself explicitly to promote faith and justice as the twin dimensions of the gospel message. The Arrupe legacy, then, is not for the faint of heart. It is, however, for those who know themselves to be weak, but who, like Arrupe, put themselves into God's hands and let God lead them where he will.

I came to know this personally when I was asked in late 1981 to go to Somalia, a country that had expelled nearly all priests several years earlier. My presence was to find out how the authorities there would react to an incoming priest. Since the plane for Mogadishu was to leave from Rome, I went to visit our stricken Fr General. When I explained that I was going to Somalia as a member of the Jesuit Refugee Service, his eyes lit up as they used to do. He half-raised himself from the couch, stuck out a trembling arm at me, and shouted, 'Go!' Go I did, and his command carried me through some scary times. His single word still energises me. I think of him, with his tiny, frail body and broad smile, as a man in whom the Holy Spirit had unrestricted freedom to operate. Like Ignatius, he was a man led by another. May his inspiration continue to fire people to do great deeds for God and God's people.

~ 8 ~

Daniel Berrigan (1921–2016)

Kevin O'Higgins SJ

One cannot level one's moral lance at every evil in
the universe. There are just too many of them. But
you can do something, and the difference between
doing something and doing nothing is everything.

– Daniel Berrigan

It may seem a little strange, or even presumptuous, to include a
recently deceased person like Daniel Berrigan in a book about
saintly people. Obviously, his death in April 2016 is much too recent
for his life to have been subjected to the careful scrutiny that usually
precedes official recognition of saintliness by the Catholic Church.
However, official acclamation frequently follows a widespread,
popular conviction that a certain individual has indeed lived an
exemplary, saint-like life. In this latter sense, Daniel Berrigan is
certainly worthy of inclusion in the present volume. In the countless
tributes that followed his passing, a common thread was the
perception that he was indeed a 'man of God' in every fibre of his
being. In the books of poetry, scripture commentary and personal
reflection which he published during his lifetime – more than fifty
in all – every page speaks of a man on fire with love for God and
God's people, especially those suffering the pain of war, poverty and
injustice of any kind.

Protest as Witness

I first became aware of Daniel Berrigan in the late 1960s, when I was in my final years of secondary school. At the time, Dan and his brother Philip, together with a like-minded group of friends collectively known as the 'Catonsville Nine', were in the news for their non-violent opposition to the war in Vietnam. Their activities, designed to draw attention to their message in dramatic fashion, included the burning of US Army draft cards and the invading of military bases. Such was their impact that an image of the Berrigans even adorned the front cover of *Time* magazine, which described them as 'rebel priests'. When Dan was sentenced to prison, following the Catonsville protest, he decided to defy the authorities symbolically by evading arrest and going on the run. Consequently, he became the first priest ever to appear on the FBI's 'most wanted' list. Given the reasons for his status as an outlaw, he wore the distinction like a badge of honour.

Back then, as a typical hard-to-impress teenager, what really struck me was the fact that I had never encountered Catholic priests like these before. I associated priests with altars, pulpits and confession boxes. It came as something of a shock, albeit a pleasant one, to see Catholic priests engaged in anti-war protests and being harassed for their actions. But Dan, especially, was very emphatic that his anti-war activities were simply an inescapable expression of his Christian commitment and priestly ministry. For me, as for many others, his anti-war, pro-peace ministry was a powerful contemporary affirmation that the Christian faith was not just concerned with subscribing to a certain set of beliefs. It was also, and primarily, about living and acting in a manner that was coherent with Christian faith and values, whatever the consequences.

A Most Faithful Jesuit

Dan Berrigan was a Jesuit, while his younger brother Phil was a member of the Josephite order. Phil later left the priesthood and married fellow activist and former religious Elizabeth McAlister; they enjoyed a happy family life. Dan continued as a Jesuit priest until his death early in 2016, just days short of his ninety-fifth birthday. Having entered the Jesuit novitiate straight from high school, his religious life spanned almost eighty years. That, in itself, is truly remarkable. When he was asked, at the age of eighty-eight, what he was most grateful for in his long life, he replied without hesitation, 'My Jesuit vocation'. His only regret was that it had taken him too long to grasp the demands of that vocation to work tirelessly for peace and in defence of the victims of all kinds of violence and injustice. On another occasion, he was asked what he might have done with his life if he had not become a Jesuit. He seemed puzzled by the question, and eventually responded, 'I have never thought about an alternative'. He couldn't even begin to imagine what a different path in life might have looked like.

Shortly before Dan's decision to engage in public acts civil of disobedience, the great Fr Pedro Arrupe had been elected Superior General of the Jesuits. Arrupe had experienced the horror of the atomic bomb in Hiroshima and was passionately opposed to violence and injustice of any kind. It was a moving moment for Dan, and a public statement of his support for him, when Arrupe, while in the United States, visited him in prison. Some months later, an Irish diocesan priest happened to encounter the Jesuit General in Rome. In the course of their brief conversation, the priest mentioned his admiration for Dan Berrigan. Fr Arrupe responded, 'Daniel Berrigan is the most faithful Jesuit of his generation'.

Family Influence

Much of the notoriety surrounding Dan and Phil Berrigan was due to the fact that they happened to be priests. Even for the secular media, seeing members of the clergy arrested and jailed was undoubtedly fascinating and newsworthy. With so much attention focused on Dan and Phil, the very similar activities of their older lay sibling, Jerry, were somewhat overshadowed. He too was a life-long educator, peace advocate and social activist. Jerry, who was just fifteen months older than Dan, died in 2015. Like his better-known younger brothers, Jerry had been arrested many times for acts of civil disobedience in opposition to war. His last arrest was in 2011, aged ninety-one.

Clearly, then, Dan Berrigan's family played a very significant role in shaping his personal values and beliefs. His conviction that the Christian faith, if it is to be authentic, must inevitably lead to action consistent with that faith had its roots in his early formation at home. The influence of his German-American mother, Frieda, and their Irish-American father, Tom, is surely crucial in this regard. Frieda Berrigan is remembered by her family as a woman of quiet, deep faith, while Tom was a lifelong socialist and union organiser. Incidentally, the Berrigan family's brand of Catholic social activism has been passed on to a third generation, with two of Phil Berrigan's children at present involved in the Catholic Worker movement. The seeds of faith and concern for justice were planted in the Berrigan home. Later, they were nourished and brought to full fruition by Dan's Jesuit formation, especially through the Spiritual Exercises of St Ignatius. It is not difficult to imagine how Dan Berrigan's poetic soul would have been moved by the moment in St Ignatius's Spiritual Exercises when the person praying is asked to imagine the Three Divine Persons observing the state of the world:

> ... men and women being born and being laid to rest, some getting married and others getting divorced, the old and the young, the rich and the poor, the happy and the sad, so many people aimless, despairing, hateful, and killing, so many undernourished, sick, and dying, so many struggling with life and blind to any meaning. With God, I can hear people laughing and crying, some shouting and screaming, some praying, others cursing.

Poet and Activist

Dan Berrigan would surely have found it easier to focus on the beautiful aspects of the world, for he had a deep sense of wonder at the whole of creation. He published his first, prize-winning book of poetry in the late 1950s, and many volumes followed in later years. Even while engaged in his most controversial acts of political disobedience, the poet and artist were never absent. Meeting him, as I was privileged to do on several occasions, he invariably came across as gentle, soft-spoken and intelligent. But this sensitive side of his personality could not mask a steely determination to do whatever he believed was necessary in order to live his life in harmony with his Christian faith and the demands of his Jesuit vocation.

What makes Dan Berrigan's long life as a Jesuit, a priest and a committed Christian so exemplary is the fact that he never wavered in his determination always to translate his faith into concrete action. Right into advanced old age, until frailty and illness obliged him to take a step back from frontline activism, he continued to participate in acts of civil disobedience in the name of peace. He also continued his involvement with the Catholic Worker Movement, founded by his great friend and mentor, Dorothy Day. In his final years, particular concerns of his were people suffering from homelessness and Aids. 'Nothing was more important to him', wrote a close friend, 'than spending a night holding the hand of a dying Aids sufferer.'

A Long Tradition

Unknown to me, when I first became aware of them back in the 1960s, Dan and Phil Berrigan were not really so exceptional. With a little more Church history under my belt, I found it easy to situate their activism and understanding of priesthood in a long tradition that stretches back to the very beginnings of Christianity. It is no exaggeration to say that, for Dan, the model he tried to emulate was Jesus himself. While there may have been few priests like him in North America or Europe in the 1960s, in poorer parts of the world it was by no means uncommon to find priests, religious and even some bishops playing a leading role in social activism. In South America, Archbishop Hélder Câmara and other Church leaders were paving the way for a new model of Church, focused on empowering ordinary people, especially the impoverished majority. In a small number of European countries, most notably France, worker priests had been active since the 1940s.

Many decades before Pope Francis urged members of the clergy to move from the sacristy to the street in order to acquire 'the smell of the sheep' and address the needs of ordinary people in the real world, worker priests were pioneering a pastoral approach that saw them exchange elegant clerical garb for factory overalls. Shortly after his ordination as priest in 1952, Dan Berrigan was sent to France, for the final year of Jesuit formation known as Tertianship. While there, he made contact with French worker priests, and their influence on him proved to be decisive.

Dan Berrigan was also young enough to be influenced by the cultural upheaval following the Second World War, a time when established authority of all kinds was being challenged and subjected to critical scrutiny. His contemporaries in the United States included the likes of Jack Kerouac, Alan Ginsberg and other leading lights of the so-called 'Beat Generation'. So, Dan Berrigan was part of a much larger movement of change within the Catholic Church and the world at large. In the early 1960s, this hunger for change both informed, and was given new impetus by, the Second Vatican Council. It is not difficult to imagine the impact on the Berrigans of a document like the Council's 'Gaudium et spes' and its declaration that, 'The joys and hopes, the grief and anguish of the people of our time, especially of those who are poor or afflicted, are the joys and hopes, the grief and anguish of the followers of Christ as well.'

Many Catholics, laity as well as clergy, responded to the Second Vatican Council by focusing on the social and political challenges of the day, and asking themselves how they should respond from the specific perspective of Christian faith. This latter point is important. As Pope Francis has frequently pointed out, the Church is not simply a benevolent society or a non-governmental organisation. While there may be many ideological reasons for wishing to change society, the Christian point of view is unique. Observing the world through the eyes of faith is a matter of trying to see it as God does, with all of its light and shadow. Then, it is a matter of striving to ensure that the light triumphs over the darkness. That, in a nutshell, is what is exemplified in the long, extraordinary life of Daniel Berrigan.

Part 3

To the Ends of the Earth

*They ought to be ready at any hour to go to any part
of the world where they may be sent.*
(Constitutions 588)

~ 9 ~

Francis Xavier (1506–52)

Philip Fogarty SJ

It is not the actual physical exertion that counts, nor the nature of the task, but the spirit of faith with which it is undertaken.

– Francis Xavier

The place was Paris, and the year was 1533. The young Francis Xavier, born to a noble family in the Spanish Kingdom of Navarre in 1506, stood listening to his roommates. One of them was another Spaniard, Ignatius from Loyola, and the other a Frenchman, Pierre Favre. They were all university students at the Collège Sainte-Barbe. 'This Ignatius', Francis thought to himself, 'is a strange man. He never seems to be ashamed to be down on the streets with the poorest of the poor, even though he has to plod along with one foot shorter than the other.' Francis knew the story behind Ignatius's bad leg: how he had been wounded in the siege of Pamplona and how, after some terrible surgeries, he had been left with a limp.

An Unsatisfied Heart

Francis, unlike Ignatius, was tall, lithe, handsome, vain and a good athlete. He was also a bright student, and was already teaching philosophy in the university. Like all students, he was constantly short of money. He felt that a nobleman like himself should be able to move about society without having to worry about such trivialities as finance, and he was constantly asking for money from his family. He would soon be finishing his studies, however, and recevied a good job offer in Pamplona. At last, he would no longer have to scrounge for money!

Francis watched Ignatius and Favre chatting. Soon enough he would be parting from them, these men who had given up worldly ambitions and decided to devote themselves completely to God's service. Thinking of separating from them, he felt a twinge of regret in himself. Slowly, over the years, he had grown close to the two of them, and would now miss them. Sadness entered his heart, as well as something akin to envy. He wondered why he felt so discontented, and then he realised the reason; his ambitions, which he had nurtured for many years, did not truly satisfy his heart.

A Decisive Change

Francis found himself reflecting on how he spent many hours on the athletic field, drinking and singing with other students in the local taverns, and rolling dice in the gaming dens. Yet, despite his popularity and success, he was not really happy. Ignatius, from the early days of their time together, used to remind him of the words of Jesus, 'What shall it profit anyone if he shall gain the whole world and lose his own soul?' Francis didn't like to hear those words, and sometimes ridiculed Ignatius as a religious fanatic. And yet he knew they made sense. Now he began to think that if God called him he would try to respond. But how could he hear God's call?

Ignatius turned to Francis. 'What are you thinking about?' he asked. 'A strange thing,' Francis answered, 'one I doubt any philosopher has ever answered or been able to answer. How does a person come to know God?' 'Saint Augustine answered that question centuries ago', Ignatius replied. 'We come to know God by love. To go to God, a person needs but to love.'

Ignatius realised that Francis was on the verge of making a major change in his life. He was moved by the fact that this man, his dear friend, was already questioning his ambitions, preparing himself to hand everything over to God. Ignatius appreciated the struggle Francis was going through, for it reminded him of the turmoil he himself had experienced many years earlier.

To Venice and Rome

Some months later, under the guidance of Ignatius, Francis made the Spiritual Exercises, thirty days of intense prayer lived in seclusion, and in the end offered everything he had – his liberty, memory, understanding and will – in the service of God. By this time, as well as Francis and Pierre, Ignatius had won over four other students to his way of life. They shared Ignatius's interest in going to the Holy Land in the hope of committing themselves to God there. The group met on 15 August 1534 in the little church of Saint Denis in Montmartre to pronounce vows of poverty and chastity. They also promised to go to the Holy Land or, failing this, to carry out the wishes of the Pope in Rome.

The little group grew bigger and, on 24 June 1537 Francis, Ignatius and several others were ordained in Venice, where they had spent some months working in hospitals and preaching at street corners. Since access to the Holy Land was impossible because of an impending war between the Turks and Venice, the companions set out for Rome to put themselves at the service of the Pope. On the way, some of them stopped off to lecture in various university cities. Francis spent some months teaching and preaching in Bologna.

While there, Francis fell ill with fever but, despite his condition, he was determined to set out for Rome with his companion, Nicolás Bobadilla, to join the others as planned. They set off on foot on the long journey from Bologna, through Florence and Siena, to Rome. Ignatius was horrified when the fever-stricken Francis arrived, and he scolded him for neglecting his health. Shortly afterwards, during the Lent of 1539, Francis participated in the discussions that eventually led to the decision to form a new religious order, the Society of Jesus. Following the election of Ignatius as the first Superior General, he revealed his plans for Francis: he wanted Francis, his old friend and roommate, to remain with him in Rome as his closest collaborator.

An Unexpected Call

In 1541 Francis was living a quiet life as secretary to Ignatius. That same year, King John III of Portugal, concerned about the state of Christianity in his dominions, requested the Pope to send missionaries to Goa. The Pope turned to Ignatius for help, and he in turn chose two of his companions for the mission: Simão Rodrigues and Nicolás Bobadilla. Bobadilla was the one who had accompanied the sick Francis on the journey from Bologna to Rome. This time, it was Bobadilla's turn to fall ill. Ignatius had to choose someone else in his place and, under pressure of time, he turned to his close friend Francis. God acts in strange ways.

Francis, aged thirty-five, soon found himself in Lisbon on board a ship bound for Goa, some 4,000 miles away. As he boarded the ship, the king's messenger handed him a papal letter appointing him *apostolic nuncio*. The king also appointed him ambassador of Portugal, but the titles meant little to Francis as he set out on a voyage that would be filled with tedium, danger and great suffering.

In September 1541, five months after his departure, Francis reached Mozambique, where he remained for about six months. Here, for the first time, he came across the evils of the slave trade. He was appalled to discover that the price for a slave was thirty pieces of silver. 'For neither more nor less Judas sold Jesus our Lord', Francis wrote in distress.

To India and Japan

Arriving in Goa in May 1542, Francis quickly became aware of the exploitation of the local people by the unscrupulous Portuguese colonists, who had settled there some thirty years earlier. 'The Europeans enrich themselves by robbery,' he wrote, 'robbery disguised under many pretexts, robbery done with impunity, with no hesitation and in full and unashamed view of all.' At one stage, Francis even wrote to the king of Portugal to protest against the abuses he saw; but in vain.

At first, Francis concentrated on amending the lives of the Portuguese colonists, but his attention was soon drawn to the plight of the local population. In October 1542, he travelled to the south coast of India and on to present-day Sri Lanka, where he spent several years among the pearl fishers, baptising converts and building churches. Early the following year, he headed off for Malacca, a port city of present-day Malaysia, and from there he went on to the Malukku islands in today's Indonesia, where he spent the next eighteen months preaching and baptising the local people.

The distances he covered on these journeys were vast. On his return to Malacca, however, he heard about another country that was even further away, Japan. Learning of the very different people who lived there, he entertained high hopes of bringing Christianity to them. First, however, he had to return to Goa, since he had been appointed provincial of the whole region, to attend to the needs of the Jesuits, who were growing in number at this time.

At last, in 1549, he set sail for Japan with three other Jesuits. On arrival, he tried to study the language, but with little success, and he mostly communicated through an interpreter. He was given permission to expound Christianity freely, but made little progress. Conversions were few and far between, and by the time he left Japan in August 1551, there were barely 1,600 Christians in the country. He was an unprofitable servant, he sadly told himself as he boarded a ship on his way back to Malacca and India.

Within Reach of China
In Japan, however, a seed of hope had been sown. He heard from the people there of yet another country, called China, which had an ancient civilization and a high culture, and whose people were held in great esteem among the Japanese. Perhaps, he thought, if he could win over China to the faith, that would be the key to converting the whole vast region of the Far East to Christianity. He found himself back in Goa in January 1552 but, within a few months, had set sail once again, this time for China itself. In August of that year, he arrived in Shangchuan, an island 14 km off the southern coast of China, and waited for the opportunity to reach the mainland.

It was not to be. A smuggler from China, who had agreed to take him the final stretch of the journey, never arrived. On 21 November, Francis began to burn with a fever, eventually becoming delirious and speaking incomprehensibly. For eight days he suffered, watched over by a loyal Chinese companion, known only as Antonio. China was just about visible on the horizon, but he was never to reach it. His last words as he lay dying were the words of his Master, 'Father, into your hands I commend my spirit'.

Francis Xavier was first buried on the Shangchuan Island, but when spring came his remains were taken to Malacca. A few years later they were removed to Goa, where they were interred in the Basilica of Bom Jesus.

An Outstanding Missionary

Francis's travels, covering enormous distances in cramped and dangerous vessels, are astonishing by any standard. Since his death, he has been regarded as one of the heroic figures of the Church's missionary efforts. He has often been portrayed as the greatest missionary since St Paul, and with justification. Today, he is sometimes criticised for his underlying theology and missionary methods, but that is to forget that he was a man of his time. Like most of his Catholic and Protestant contemporaries, he believed that all who died without being baptised would be lost. This is what determined the priority he gave to baptism in his missionary work. It is also what gave a great sense of urgency to his ministry.

Over time, Francis Xavier learned a great deal from the people he met and, as he came to understand them better, he adapted his approach considerably. Fr Adolfo Nicolás, the former Superior General of the Jesuits, has spoken of this:

> Francis was a man on fire with zeal to spread the good news of the gospel. When he arrived in India his attitude to the great religions of the East was confrontational and very negative. He made some mistakes because he was, to some extent, a prisoner of his own worldview. By the time he reached Japan he had begun to change as a result of meeting – really

meeting – people who were very different from him. In these meetings, he began to realise that he was not totally right. He began to listen, to respect and to admire. As a missionary, he changed. In India, he had confronted the Hindu leaders and spoken harshly of their religion. In Japan it was different.

Francis Xavier experienced the great variety of languages, faiths, cultures and living conditions, as few had experienced them before him. He first saw this maddening variety as a hindrance to his missionary efforts before sensing, progressively, that this varied and complicated world was the one in which God was indeed living and working, and where he could be found.

~ 10 ~

Edmund Campion (1540–81)

David Stewart SJ

> If these my offers be refused, and my endeavours
> can take no place, and I, having run thousands of
> miles to do you good, shall be rewarded with rigour,
> I have no more to say but to recommend your case
> and mine to Almighty God, the Searcher of Hearts,
> who send us his grace, and set us at accord before the
> day of payment, to the end we may at last be friends
> in heaven, when all injuries shall be forgotten.
>
> – Edmund Campion

People discovering the story of Edmund Campion for the first time might wonder if they have encountered a figure too heroic and too brave for this world, a figure beyond credibility. Those more familiar with him, however, are likely to see the human being: someone blessed with enormous intellectual gifts and personal qualities but like any of us drawn this way and that by the competing claims upon him. Heroism was not inevitably his, at least to begin with. There must have been many moments when he hesitated, wondering which way he should turn. There were many choices and opportunities open to him.

It does not do him justice, then, to imagine him simply as the gifted child of a middle-class London family who, in young adulthood, converted to the former faith of his country and who then refused to compromise his beliefs, thereby losing both his career and his life. This is all true, but the reality is much subtler, more nuanced.

Outstanding Scholar

The son of a London bookseller, from an early age Campion was well known for his intellectual brilliance. At the age of thirteen, he was chosen to make a speech of welcome to Mary Tudor when, as queen, she visited his school. He was awarded a scholarship to St John's College, Oxford, when only fifteen years old, and became a fellow by the age of seventeen. He quickly became an outstanding figure in the university, influential and charismatic, attracting admiring students who hung on his every word. Sometimes they imitated his style and mannerisms, even calling themselves 'Campionists'. He seemed destined for a stellar academic career. The world was at his feet.

As Campion was establishing his reputation at Oxford, great changes in the university and the country were taking place. Elizabeth I, who occupied the throne from 1558 until her death in 1603, presided over a country and a Church still grappling with the consequences of Henry VIII's break with Rome. The dissolution of the monasteries had a severe impact on the country. The ransacking of other major institutions added to the uncertainty of the times, for most of these institutions, including Oxford, had for generations been intrinsically linked with the Church. Most students of the time were preparing for ecclesiastical careers, while almost all important officials were ordained priests.

With all signs of popery abolished, the Mass made illegal and a large proportion of the clergy dispossessed, it became ever more difficult for the authorities to find leaders in the new situation. Many had fled overseas. When, in 1566, Elizabeth came to Oxford on an elaborate six-day visit, Campion was chosen to make a formal speech of welcome, which he did in elegant Ciceronian Latin. Later, he led a public debate in the presence of the sovereign. Impressed by his charm and erudition, the queen and her advisers recognised in him the qualities of a future leader. With his many notable gifts, Campion was exactly the kind of person they needed. From that moment prestige and power could have been his.

Inner Struggle

At the time, however, Campion's intention was to pursue a life of study and teaching, for which he was well suited. He knew that this would only be possible if he proceeded towards orders in the Church of England and consequently, in 1568, he put himself forward for ordination as a deacon. This decision involved him taking the Oath of Supremacy, swearing allegiance to the monarch as head of State and Church. He was now a step closer to fulfilling his heart's desire.

Yet he had misgivings, and he found himself wavering in his convictions. Reading the Fathers of the Church had led him to think deeply about his faith, and he found himself strongly attracted to the claims of Rome and the papacy. Unwisely, perhaps, he did not keep his interests to himself. As a lover of debate and principled argument, he did little to hide his questioning. His Catholic sympathies became common knowledge in the university, and some of his confrères demanded that he make a clear and unambiguous statement of his sympathies. He resisted the pressure for as long as he could, in the hope, no doubt, that the many powerful friends he had in Oxford would be able to protect him and enable him to live in peace with his books.

Joining the Jesuits

The controversy did not go away. Campion's failure to declare his true position continued to hound him and, under pressure, he left Oxford in 1569 and moved to colonial Dublin, where he finally became a Roman Catholic. If he was hoping for a quiet life in the Irish capital, he was to be sorely disappointed, for his sojourn in Ireland offered him little respite from the pressures of the time. Tension was mounting between London and Rome. In 1570, Pope Pius V declared Elizabeth a heretic and excommunicated her. Until then, Elizabeth had not strictly enforced her anti-Catholic legislation, but now the persecution began to intensify. Hostility to Catholics throughout England and among the ruling classes in Ireland notably increased. Sensing the danger, Campion fled to Douai in the Low Countries.

Shortly before his arrival, Cardinal William Allen had established the English College in Douai, a seminary for the training of priests who would minister in England. There must have been jubilation in the college when Campion, this outstanding scholar, presented himself as a student for the priesthood. To the many Catholic acquaintances he met there, it must have seemed that Campion had discovered another way into the academic world he so loved. But something had shifted in Campion's soul, and he began to realise that his dream of an academic life was fading. Something more was about to be demanded of him.

Within a few years of his arrival in Douai, Campion found himself drawn to the Jesuits, the new and innovative religious order founded by Ignatius Loyola and his companions in 1540, the year of Campion's birth. Campion determined to join this new company, and in 1573 he walked barefoot to Rome where he presented himself for admission. Since there was no possibility of a novitiate in England, Campion was assigned to the Austrian Province. He began his novitiate in Prague and continued it in Brno. He then went on to study in Vienna and in the Jesuit College in Prague. Ordained in 1578, he taught for a short time in that same college.

A Fugitive in England

In 1580, Pope Gregory XIII, concerned about the situation of Catholics in England, requested that two Jesuits be sent on a perilous mission. The two chosen, Frs Robert Persons and Edmund Campion, were soon joined by a third, Br Ralph Emerson. They met in Rome to plan their course of action, but even before they set out their intentions had become known to Elizabeth's spies. Disguised as a jewel merchant, Campion arrived in Dover in June 1580 and quickly made covert contact with some leading Catholics. He soon learned of the ever-present danger, with government agents on special watch for any signs of Catholic resurgence. From the start, the three Jesuits went underground and remained out of sight as much as possible.

Now a hunted figure, Campion had to keep moving around the country as surreptitiously as possible, while offering solace to those loyal to the old faith. Government priest-hunters, including the notoriously vicious Richard Topcliffe, were on his trail. Rumours were circulating that his mission had a political end in view. To counter this charge, Campion boldly – and perhaps imprudently – issued a refutation, addressed to the Privy Council. This powerful document, which became known as *Campion's Brag*, was widely distributed throughout the country. In it he declared that his mission was 'of free cost to preach the gospel, to minister the sacraments, to instruct the simple, to reform sinners, to confute errors – in brief to cry a spiritual alarm against foul vice and proud ignorance, wherewith many of my dear countrymen are abused.' He went on, 'I never had mind, and am strictly forbidden by our Father that sent me, to deal in any respect with matter of state or policy of this realm, as things which appertain not to my vocation, and from which I gladly restrain and sequester my thoughts.' He ended with hopes for a better time 'when all injuries will be forgotten'.

Shortly afterwards, Campion wrote another work, entitled *Decem Rationes*, this time in Latin. Aimed at the academic world, it made the case in ten arguments for the validity of the Catholic faith. It was printed at Stonor House, an old mansion in Oxfordshire owned by the recusant Stonor family, where both Campion and Persons sometimes stayed. Many of the 400 copies of this tract were left on the benches of St Mary's Church in Oxford University, causing a stir among the academics and an intensification of the search for the fugitive Jesuit. Stonor House, and the room where this document was printed, may be visited to this day.

Imprisonment and Trial
Campion continued his clandestine ministry, but not for long. In July 1581, as he celebrated Mass at the home of a family in Berkshire,

an undercover government agent was among the members of the congregation. The authorities were alerted and came to arrest him. They found him, along with two other priests, in a 'priest hole', one of many such hiding-places that had been constructed in Catholic houses around the country to shelter priests in times of danger.

He was taken to London and imprisoned in the Tower. The cell he was given for the first few days was so small that he was unable either to stand or lie down. Soon, however, there was a change of strategy. Efforts were made to entice Campion to renounce his faith with offers of freedom and speedy promotion. At one stage, he was secretly taken by boat on the Thames to meet Queen Elizabeth, who heard him repeat his reasons for being in England and acknowledge her as the lawful sovereign in all temporal matters. Both of them must have remembered their previous meeting in Oxford, and regretted the changed circumstances of their present encounter.

When persuasion failed, the tortures began, and for four months he endured appalling treatment in the Tower of London. His fingernails were torn out and he was subjected several times to most extreme torment of all, the rack. On four occasions, still weakened from the torture, he was made to stand – without preparation or notes of any kind – and engage in public disputes with opposing divines, in the hope of undoing his reputation.

At his trial in Westminster Hall, he was so weakened that he could not lift his hand to take the oath. The trial was designed to show the populace that he was arraigned, not because of his faith, but because he was complicit in plotting against the crown, and so he was charged with treason. As before, and despite his weakened condition, Campion dazzled with the clarity of his arguments and the serenity of his demeanour, but the die was already cast. Found guilty of treason, he was dragged through the streets of London to the infamous Tyburn, where he was executed with two others on 1 December 1581. That date is now marked as the feast day of St Edmund Campion.

An Enduring Legacy

If we come to Campion's story for the first time we can easily miss the gradual conversion, not only intellectual but also spiritual, that marked his forty-one years of life. If he was a hero, he was a reluctant one. He never lost the taste for debate and disputation. His wonderful intellect never dimmed, even in extreme suffering. He retained his attractive personality to the end. There were many opportunities for advancement open to him, yet he knowingly rejected a glamorous, glittering career for a higher cause.

His best-known biographer, Evelyn Waugh, ends his work with a vivid description of the crowd at Tyburn, revelling in the bloodthirsty scene on the day of Campion's execution. In that throng was one Henry Walpole, a bright young man who harboured Catholic sympathies but who knew enough to keep quiet and out of trouble. Some of the martyr's blood splattered Walpole's tunic. At that moment, his life was changed forever. He left for the continent to become a priest and a Jesuit, returned to England, was arrested and, thirteen years after Campion, died a similar death on the gallows at York. In this way, the words of *Campion's Brag*, echoing the *Acts of the Apostles*, were confirmed: 'If it is of God, it cannot be withstood'.

~ 11 ~

John Ogilvie (1579–1615)

David Stewart SJ

> In all that concerns the king, I will be slavishly
> obedient; if any attack his temporal power, I will
> shed my last drop of blood for him. But in the
> things of spiritual jurisdiction which a king unjustly
> seizes, I cannot and must not obey.
>
> – John Ogilvie

Whenever John Ogilvie, the European traveller, gazed out of his window in Germany, Moravia or France, he may well have found himself dreaming of his native Banffshire in Scotland, where he had been raised. If he did have such wistful daydreams of home, however, they would not have lasted too long. John had long since left his native land and was destined for the road, travelling widely in Europe in search of education and searching too for his calling in life.

In due time, as we will see, his earthly journey ended back in the relatively new nation of Scotland, not in his own part of it, but in Glasgow. Glasgow in those days was already developing extensive trading and cultural links with Europe, and was becoming noted for its international outlook and cosmopolitan feel. Ogilvie's execution in 1615 was carried out at the busy intersection of Glasgow Cross, still near the centre of the city today, in what is now known as the Merchant City district. As his death approached, we are told that John threw his rosary into the crowd, where it was caught by a Hungarian visitor to the city – further evidence of the growing international links in those heady days of the early seventeenth century. John Ogilvie can therefore be considered a saint, not just for his native Scotland, but also for Europe. He can be a saint for our time as well, as we shall see.

Family Background

John was born in 1579 into a well-off Calvinist family in Drum-na-Keith, in north-east Scotland. His father, Walter, a respected landowner, possessed a large estate in that lovely rolling and fertile landscape. Situated in the Highlands, in the north of Scotland, Drum-na-Keith lies to the east of the rugged Cairngorm Mountain range. This is a pleasant land of big skies and solid stone buildings set in tidy towns. As it rolls down to the North Sea and Moray Firth it is a softer landscape than the Cairngorms, although it can still be snowy in winter.

John's family on his father's side had been Calvinist since the early days of the Scottish Reformation. His mother, Agnes, who died when he was only three years old, was a Catholic, and two of his uncles on her side, George and William Elphinstone, had themselves been Jesuits. That branch of the family tree was most likely related to the noted Bishop William Elphinstone of Aberdeen, who in 1495 had founded a university there.

The sixteenth-century Scottish Reformation, almost parallel to, but not the same as that of England, had pushed Catholicism to the margins of the country, driving the few remaining priests either overseas or underground. Walter Ogilvie made sure that his son was brought up in the Presbyterian faith, a severe form of which had tightened its grip on the country by the time John approached his teenage years. John's father was also determined that his son should receive a good education, and so in 1792 he sent him, at the age of thirteen, to Helmstedt in Germany. Subsequently John travelled extensively around the continent, exposing him to the era's religious and political turmoil, and leading him in time to face the deeper issues of his own commitment.

Religious Turmoil

The religious identity of the post-Reformation Scots nation was marked by a lot of uncertainty. It was a tormented period of religious and political insecurity, during which there were several fluctuations, now towards Episcopalianism, now towards Presbyterianism. All the while, the skilled political philosopher King James VI knew well how to play one faction off against another. In 1603, the two crowns of Scotland and England would be united, although the two nations would not become a single political entity for more than a century. James's policy had seen him dabble with the idea of state-appointed bishops, a policy that infuriated the Presbyterian camp, which had no tolerance for anything suggesting episcopal authority. In this situation, Roman Catholics found themselves beleaguered from both sides. In time, John Ogilvie would come to repudiate any claim by the monarch to dictate anyone's religious belief. It was for this conviction that he was killed by the state.

Confounding his father's hopes for his son, John began to question his Calvinist upbringing as he travelled throughout Europe. The religious turmoil of the time was inescapable, and we can imagine this imaginative and bright young itinerant scholar immersing himself in current affairs, keen to understand what was going on around him. As he studied in various places, John broadened his experience and expanded his mind. He had acquired a good knowledge of several European languages, and so was able to converse easily with fellow students and lecturers. Gradually he became convinced that he could no longer accept the Calvinist doctrine of predestination, that God willed only some, not all, to be saved. For John, the apostle Paul's belief in the Church as the body of Christ, to which all are invited, became a central tenet. In 1597 he became a Roman Catholic at Leuven, in present-day Belgium, and two years later he joined the Society of Jesus. In 1610 he was ordained priest in Paris, the city where Calvin himself had studied less than a century earlier.

Jesuit Formation

John's formation as a Jesuit, which he received over a number of years in several places, was both spiritual and intellectual. Rooted in the spirituality of St Ignatius Loyola, who had founded the order almost forty years before John was born, this training aimed at equipping the young Jesuit with the tools of discernment, by fostering an inner freedom from self-centred attractions. This inner freedom Ignatius called 'indifference', a word that can easily give rise to misunderstanding. Rather than any kind of disinterested attitude towards created reality, Ignatius wished his followers to become aware of their own 'disordered attachments' and, having rid themselves of these as far as possible, to become freer to respond to whatever call the Spirit prompted in their heart. Indifference, for Ignatius, meant interior freedom.

Growth in this kind of freedom is central to the Spiritual Exercises, which John, as a novice, made as a silent thirty-day retreat. Like everyone who experiences the Spiritual Exercises, whether in the thirty-day format or over an extended time in everyday life, he would have come to an awareness of himself as a loved sinner, one who is not only forgiven but called and sent. The Spiritual Exercises plunge the retreatant into the ministry of Christ himself, inviting us to contemplate how Christ 'laboured' – Ignatius's precisely chosen word – all the way to the cross, and still labours in the world today. Various meditations and contemplations are designed to expose those areas where inner freedom is weak, opening the heart to greater generosity and service.

John imbibed all of this with enthusiasm. Many Scots, it is said, are noted for doing nothing by half, for good or for ill, and John was certainly among them. Allied to his innate adventurousness and daring spirit, the spirituality he discovered as a Jesuit became a powerful admixture in his life. Far from suppressing his personality, it allowed his strength of character to flourish. Following his ordination, it eventually prompted him to ask his Jesuit superiors for permission to return to his native land to minister to the beleaguered Catholics there.

Torture, Trial and Death

He was refused, but with characteristic persistence he continued to make his case, and in the end won the day. Disguised as a horse dealer, under the alias of John Watson, Ogilvie returned secretly to Scotland in November 1613. His priority was to encourage and support Catholics imprisoned by the state, and to celebrate Mass with them – all illegal activities, of course. John, having been absent from his native land for twenty-two years, was betrayed by a false friend and arrested after only eleven months of ministry. The Protestant Archbishop Spottiswoode of St Andrews, who enjoyed royal favour, charged John with the words, 'You would do well not to say your Masses in a reformed city'.

His arraignment, torture and trial were vicious. At one stage, in an attempt to make him reveal the names of other Catholics, he was kept awake for eight days and nine nights. Another torture, known as 'the boots', involved the wearing of shackles that forced the very bone marrow from his legs. Five months of cruelty did not weaken his spirit, however. He amazed his tormentors by responding with fortitude, even humour, through it all. When asked if he was afraid to die, he is reputed to have answered, 'I fear death as much as you do your dinner'. Finally, he was convicted of high treason for refusing to accept the king's religious jurisdiction. On 10 March 1615, aged thirty-six, John Ogilvie was paraded through the streets of Glasgow and hanged at Glasgow Cross. His remains were thrown into a pauper's grave outside the city, the location of which has never been discovered. In 1976, Pope Paul VI declared John Ogilvie to be Scotland's first canonised saint for over 700 years.

A Lesson for Our Time

We honour John Ogilvie now, over 400 years since his execution, as a martyr for religious freedom. He died with a prayer on his lips, a powerful reminder of our need to protect religious freedom in our own time, when once again that very freedom is coming under threat. John was put to death for refusing to acknowledge the supremacy the king claimed in spiritual matters and for refusing to apostatise.

Pressure on religious tolerance is once again emerging in our day as a serious threat. It is an aspect of that 'globalisation of indifference' that Pope Francis has repeatedly emphasised, a development in our world that is rooted in individualism and selfishness, intolerance and bigotry.

John Ogilvie's was a local struggle in a small European state; the martyrdom of contemporary Christians is displayed on a global screen. Yet, across four centuries and two very different contexts, a common thread runs through them both. Religious affiliation is used as an excuse for inhuman barbarity. In our own time, as in John's, Christians everywhere reel in dismay at the outrages and persecutions visited upon fellow Christians. The difference is that we can all see these horrific murders now as the images are callously posted online. If we are to learn the lessons of our history, we must make sure to eliminate all forms of religious intolerance, whether exercised against Christians, Jews or Muslims, from our society, or else pay the price of our failures.

We must also be alert to another, less obvious and less shocking, form of intolerance that lurks in our society as well. Voices are frequently raised today denouncing faith as something regressive, and ridiculing people of faith as bigots. These are voices that seem unaware of the irony of their own position. In the time of John Ogilvie, similar charges would have been heard in a Glaswegian accent directed against Catholics. At stake in these different contexts is religious freedom, civil tolerance and the acceptance of difference. Our need to reflect on these realities is just as urgent in our own time as it was in John Ogilvie's short life.

~ 12 ~

Peter Claver (1581–1654)

David Gaffney SJ

> We must speak to people with our hands by giving,
> before we try to speak to them with our lips.
>
> – Peter Claver

S old into slavery in order to man the plantations in South America in the 1600s, the unfortunates seized from western Africa saw one in three of their companions die during the horrific two-month voyage to Cartagena in Colombia. This was considered an acceptable level of loss by the slave-ship captains. Fed and watered once a day, and chained to one another in batches of six by neck and foot, they were often told that they were on their way to be killed by the foreigner. Finally emerging from the stinking, boiling hold of the ship, imagine their surprise to be greeted by a sallow face which this time was not scowling, but smiling. The face belonged to Peter Claver, who had come to the port to hug and clothe the new arrivals and to shower them with gifts.

The Slave Trade

This witness to Christ's love for the so-called 'lowest of the low' had discovered a call within a call. Born in 1581 in Verdú, Catalonia, about fifty miles from Barcelona, Peter was twenty when he joined the new order of priests and brothers, founded in 1540 by Ignatius

Loyola from Spain's Basque country. Just as one modern founder called his followers the 'little brothers of Jesus', in a similar way Ignatius used refer to his group as the little band, or company, of Jesus; and this Society of Jesus is today best known as the Jesuits. The Jesuits felt called to go to whatever part of the world was most in need of hearing the good news about Jesus. And so, in increasing numbers, they followed the explorers to, among other places, the New World. At the prompting of the saintly Jesuit brother Alphonsus Rodriguez, porter in the Jesuit college in Majorca, Peter offered himself for the mission in South America.

Peter was not the first to respond in a heroic fashion to the plight of slaves, of course. Centuries before, when Muslim ships would pounce on the coastal towns of southern Europe and carry off thousands into slavery, two religious orders were founded specifically to help with the redemption of slaves. These orders raised funds to pay the ransoms demanded, and their members frequently went personally on ransoming missions. They vowed to remain in chains as hostages themselves, until their companions should arrive with the ransom demanded for the captives' release.

With the discovery of the New World by Europeans in the fifteenth and sixteenth centuries, a new and lucrative slave trade developed. It is estimated that, during the sixty- to seventy-year period, when the colonial authorities sanctioned the importation of slaves in the regions of Cartagena and Veracruz, 1,000,000 Africans arrived in total. That suggests that between 10,000 and 15,000 slaves arrived annually. Prone to skin diseases and plague, many of them had horrendous sores and putrid ulcers upon landing. Some attempts were made to arrange pastoral care for these uprooted souls, but these largely came to nothing. The locals complained that the stench caused them their stomachs to retch.

A Practical Response

In reality, then, the practical work of caring for the slaves was left to a few brave spirits, with Peter as the outstanding leader among them. He saw himself continuing the work of an earlier pioneering missionary, Fr Alonso de Sandoval SJ, who had worked among the slaves and had published a book decrying their inhumane treatment. In his own ministry, Peter relied for help mainly on his staff of African interpreters. Once a ship was sighted, he would begin to beg for food to bring to the slaves. Then, on board with his translators, he would offer them whatever food he had gathered, and try to ease their pain and offer them the comfort of his kindness. It is said that he would not leave a ship until everyone present had received a measure of care. Many saints have, on occasion, kissed the sores of the sick, but with Claver this was a regular occurrence.

Slaves requesting baptism were given full instruction, and a splendid ceremony was laid on for them. There was also opportunity for after-care. Peter would follow his converts to the plantations to which they were sent, encouraging them to live a Christian life, and entreating their masters to treat them humanely. In the local Jesuit church, of which he had charge, and on parish missions in the surrounding countryside, Peter carried the same message to anyone who would listen. 'No mother was ever as watchful for her children,' remarked one of his companions, 'as Peter Claver was for his converts'.

Living Images of Christ
When we look for the inner motivation which powered Peter's life, we have to begin with his background. The civil society in which he grew up was highly stratified, with a code of honour that separated a ruling class – to whose lower rungs his impoverished family may have aspired – from everyone else. This whole social framework was the imaginative matrix on which the basic Christian message, in all its paradox, was communicated. Jesus, the Lord of heaven, had abased himself in order to become one of us on earth. By emptying himself and joining the 'little ones' of this world, he had inverted all known categories. Since the Saviour had offered his life for the least of humanity, Peter was convinced that he could not shrink from putting himself, in turn, at the disposal of those most despised. Peter would surely have agreed with another Jesuit of that time who

said of the slave trade, 'It is a greater sin to force an African into slavery than to profane a crucifix; because a crucifix is a dead image of Christ, but an African is a living one.'

This insight on its own would have been strong enough to drive Peter's lifelong devotion to the slaves. It is probably what animated his prayer – he prayed for more hours each day than he slept – and his prayer in turn would have animated his thirty-eight years of unrelenting ministry, beginning with his ordination at the age of thirty-six. He died in 1654, having finally caught the plague a few years earlier. Fittingly, when Pope Leo XIII canonised him in 1888, he canonised at the same time the source of his inspiration, Alphonsus Rodriguez. On that occasion, the Pope remarked that Claver's was the life that most reminded him of Christ's. His feast day – until recently celebrated only by Jesuits – has now been extended to the universal Church, and is celebrated on 10 September.

A Change of Attitude

Peter has sometimes been accused of simply accepting slavery – a crime widespread at the time – and doing little to reform the structures of society facilitating it. There is some truth in this. We should realise, however, that an activist can frequently prepare the ground for reform, without living long enough to see the reform given institutional shape. Often it is individuals, prepared to accompany suffering minorities, who raise the public consciousness to a level that eventually issues in radical change.

There are many examples of this kind of heroic accompaniment in our own time. We remember, for example, those who walk with prisoners on death row in countries where the death penalty still exists. Or we think of those who walked with Aids sufferers when that disease was a death sentence. Or we think of those who spend time with the destitute on the pavements of the world's poorest cities, or those who help victims of abuse recover their dignity, or those who reach out to the victims of trafficking today. In some cases, such people are able to effect practical change in the way society is organised. But very often they are individuals – like Peter

Claver – who are deeply moved by what immediately meets their gaze, and who are determined to neutralise this obscenity here and now.

The big advances Christianity effected for civilization, it has been said, came about because Christian influence was first able to create a changed attitude and climate of thought. When Peter Claver found great crowds queuing for confession in his church in Cartagena, he was in the position of bringing the slaves among them to the front of the queue. He had come a long way from the day when, as a young man, he had first spotted branded slaves exhibited for sale like cattle.

~ 13 ~

Jacques Berthieu (1838–96)

Thomas Casey SJ

> God knows how much I still love the soil of my
> country and the beloved land of the Auvergne. And
> yet God has given me the grace to love even more
> these uncultivated fields of Madagascar, where I can
> catch only a few souls for our Lord.
>
> – Jacques Berthieu

We instinctively like people with big hearts, people who are full of
life and passion, always ready to give a helping hand, and who reach
out to others with compassion and love. But what about someone
who wants instead to have a small heart? Isn't that a rather miserly
way to approach life? Isn't it a stingy way to live? And how could
a saint, of all people, desire such a petty way of being for himself?
Well, that's what the French Jesuit saint, who was canonised in
2012, wrote about himself: he wanted to have a small heart. The
precise words Jacques Berthieu used are: 'I don't want to possess any
land but a small heart...'

Receiving All from God
Jacques Berthieu wrote those words the very year he entered the
Jesuit novitiate, the year he turned thirty-five. He was already a
priest at this stage; in fact he had been ordained priest nine years

beforehand. But after serving in his diocese for almost a decade, he felt it was time to test out his call to become a missionary, so he applied to join the Jesuits.

If he only wanted a small heart, and that was the end of the story, his wish would certainly sound ungenerous, but crucially, Jacques added something else. The words that I have quoted thus far form only the first half of a sentence, and the second half of the sentence is vitally important. Here is the whole thing: 'I don't want to possess any land, but a small heart to love people in the divine heart of Jesus.' This is the full story: Jacques wanted to be small so that Jesus could be big. He wanted to be tiny so that the huge heart of Jesus could have the necessary space to be the driving force in his life.

Some words of St Thérèse of Lisieux may help to explain better what Jacques was driving at. Thérèse was born in 1873, the same year Jacques Berthieu entered the Jesuit novitiate. She died in 1897, a year after he was martyred. These two saints never met; she was from Normandy, he was from the Auvergne, and these places are about 600 km apart. There was no contact between them, yet we know that this extraordinary young woman, who was later declared patron saint of the missions, constantly prayed and made sacrifices for all missionaries. Her prayers and sacrifices, therefore, would have also benefited Jacques Berthieu. A woman of wisdom way beyond her years, she once offered these precious words: 'To remain a child before God means to recognise our nothingness, to expect everything from God'.

I know that for my part, if I recognise my nothingness, I'm tempted to give up then and there. Why? Because I imagine I can do nothing, full stop. In other words, I forget the second part of Thérèse's advice: 'to expect everything from God'. I overlook this crucial point, and end up becoming anxious in the face of my own nothingness. But when I stop to think about it, I realise that nothingness isn't something I should bother paying attention to at all. After all, I don't even stop to think about insignificant things, so why should I pause to think about nothingness? Why look at nothing? Why get preoccupied by nothing? In fact, the point of recognising my nothingness is not to become fixated on it, but to concentrate on God instead. God is everything, God is all, so God should get all my attention. Thérèse realised this, and so did Jacques Berthieu.

Total Self-Giving

It was because Jacques didn't rely on himself that he could give so much more than it seemed humanly possible to give. In a letter addressed to all Jesuits on the occasion of Jacques Berthieu's canonisation, the Jesuit General Father Adolfo Nicolás declared that, 'The total and irreversible gift of his life in the following of Christ was at the heart of his commitment.' 'Total' and 'irreversible' are two strong adjectives which give a sense of how massive Jacque's self-giving was. In describing his own missionary work, Berthieu said, 'This is what it means to be a missionary: to make oneself all things to all people, both interiorly and externally; to be responsible for everything, people, animals, and things, and all this in order to gain souls, with a large and generous heart.'

Jacques didn't experience spectacular success during his years as a missionary in Madagascar, and yet he wasn't discouraged, because he knew it wasn't about him; it was about God. He wrote, 'The mission progresses, even though the fruit is still a matter of hope in some places, and hardly visible in others. But what does it matter, so long as we are good sowers? God will give growth when the time comes.'

And Berthieu did sow. He helped people to hone their agricultural skills, to develop irrigation systems, to create gardens and to construct buildings. Alonside these efforts to improve the quality of the people's material life, he also imparted the truths of faith. Although he wasn't a professor and he was no intellectual, he studied the catechism assiduously so that he could share the riches of his faith in an informed and clear manner. A young teacher once noticed that Jacques had his catechism open as they both rode on horseback through the countryside, and every so often would read a few lines when he had the opportunity. When the young man asked him why, Jacques answered, 'My son, the catechism is a book one can never understand deeply enough, since it contains all of Catholic doctrine.'

Jacques was also a man of deep prayer. As one eyewitness remarked, 'I have seen no other Father remain so long before the Blessed Sacrament. Whenever we looked for him, we were sure to find him there.' Whenever he was seen walking, he was always carrying the rosary beads – the rosary was his favourite prayer – or a breviary.

Capture and Martyrdom

Before he even left France to go on the missions, Jacques had made a special consecration of himself to the Sacred Heart at Paray-le-Monial, and he spread the message of the Sacred Heart among the people of Madagascar. Because he relied on God for everything, he knew that he would receive the grace to give everything, even – if necessary – his very life. And that's what happened in the midst of the *Menalamba* (Red Shawl) uprising against French colonial rule. As he was a foreigner and French, Jacques was targeted in this popular rebellion. He was captured on the 8 June 1896. Having been struck on the forehead with a machete, Jacques, bleeding heavily, was dragged on a six-mile trek by a group of armed men. All during this ordeal he kept reciting his favourite prayer, the rosary. When they reached the village of Ambohitra, they stoned him, then took the handkerchief from his bleeding head, soaked it in mud and dirty water, and wrapped it around his head shouting, 'Behold the king of the Europeans' – uncanny echoes of Christ's Passion!

A platoon of six men armed with guns was called in. Two of them took aim at him, but missed. Then one of their leaders came over to the kneeling priest and said, 'Give up your hateful religion. Do not mislead the people anymore, and we will make you our counsellor and our chief, and we will spare you.' When he refused, the men fired and killed him.

One of Jacque's favourite lines from the gospel had always been, 'Don't be afraid of those who kill the body, but can't kill the soul' *(Mt.10:28)*. He was a man of hope, and he knew that death wasn't the end. That's why, when giving catechism classes, he liked to speak of the Resurrection. To make the message of the Resurrection clear in the minds of his listeners, he often said, 'Even if you are eaten by a crocodile, you will rise again'. Perhaps this example showed that he knew something of what would eventually happen to him. After he was killed, two villagers dragged his body to the local river, but when others came to look for his remains shortly afterwards, there was nothing to be found. Had his body been snatched by a crocodile? Such a turn of events wouldn't have troubled at all a man with such a deep-rooted faith in the Resurrection.

A Deep Inner Life

Like St Thérèse, whom I mentioned earlier, St Jacques Berthieu was not concerned about how his limited human resources might rise to the challenges of the huge mission to which he had been called. He knew that God was everything, and that the only thing God asked for was his assent, his 'yes', to the divine will. Once he said this yes, God's grace entered his heart and his life bore (and continues to bear) great fruit. Jacques's simple and saintly soul reminds me of the description the famous Jesuit theologian Karl Rahner once gave of self-giving Jesuits he had known in his own life: 'I still see around me, living in many of my companions, a readiness for disinterested service carried out in silence, a readiness for prayer, for abandonment to the incomprehensibility of God, for the calm acceptance of death in whatever form it may come, for total dedication to the following of Christ crucified.'

Since he had surrendered himself fully to the utter incomprehensibility of God, Jacques was enveloped in that same silence of service, which went so deep that he was ready to calmly accept whatever came. It's not surprising that he had a great devotion to St Joseph. Like the foster father of Jesus, Jacques was a quiet man whose life speaks with a disarming eloquence. Although the events around his martyrdom were painful and spectacular, everything that preceded it was humdrum and routine. His was not a life full of drama or fanfare. The true heart of his commitment was shrouded in an aura of mystery, in those long hours spent in prayer before the Blessed Sacrament or walking tranquilly while clutching his rosary beads in his hand. It was from this deep inner life that he received the strength to make the momentous choice of laying down his life for Christ. It was because he immersed himself so much in the heart of Jesus that he was able to give so much more than he could ever have given with his own little heart.

Jacques Berthieu was canonised on 21 October 2012, as the Year of Faith was drawing to a close. The purpose of the Year of Faith was to invite Catholics to surrender their lives to Jesus Christ in a deeper and more sustained way. St Jacques Berthieu epitomised this loving kind of surrender. His feast day is celebrated on 8 June, the same day he was martyred.

~ 14 ~

Walter Ciszek (1904–84)

Anthony Corcoran SJ

I knew that I must abandon myself completely to the will of the Father and live from now on in this spirit of self-abandonment to God. And I did it. I can only describe the experience as a sense of 'letting go', giving over totally my last effort or even any will to guide the reins of my own life. It is all too simply said, yet that one decision has affected every subsequent moment of my life. I have to call it a conversion … It was at once a death and a resurrection.

– Walter Ciszek

O n the morning of 12 October 1963, Walter Ciszek arrived in the United States, having spent twenty-three years in the Soviet Union. An enthusiastic crowd waited to greet him. Some wondered if the man who was to step off the airplane could really be the same person they had last seen all those years ago. Many had presumed that his life – like the lives of millions of others – had had been snuffed out somewhere in the notorious gulags of the Stalinist regime. Sixteen years before his return, his Jesuit brothers had been instructed to offer Mass for the repose of his soul.

Unbroken by the Gulag

Yet here he was walking down the steps of the plane, before being ushered into the immigration office to present his documents. His arrival touched the hearts and imaginations of countless people, many of which had prayed fervently for years for his safe return. Television viewers later had the opportunity of watching his arrival on the news, intrigued by this man who had crossed the border from Poland into the Soviet Union in 1940, where he was arrested and convicted as a spy. Having served five years' internment in the dreaded Lubyanka Prison in Moscow, Ciszek was sentenced to fifteen years of hard labour in the penal camps of Northern Siberia. Released under severe restrictions, for the final years of his exile he worked quietly as a mechanic in eastern Siberia, living and toiling among ordinary Soviet citizens. Through all of his trials he contrived to say Mass whenever he could, to offer a listening ear and sacramental support to his fellow believers, and to share something of his faith with those who had none.

As his story gained circulation, what people found most remarkable about Walter Ciszek was not the litany of horrors that he had endured for so many years. Other people had suffered similar and even worse fates. What stood out in his story was the fact that, as he says himself, he had returned as if from the dead, 'but unbroken, not brainwashed, and with a heart filled with compassion for the people to whom his whole adult life as a priest has been consecrated'. He would later remark that what most people wanted to know was how he had survived the years of severe trials. His response, he admitted, was certain to disappoint some: 'My answer has always been – and can only be – that I survived on the basis of the faith others may find too simple and naïve.'

Walter Ciszek wrote two powerful and accessible books about his experience in the gulag, *With God in Russia* and *He Leadeth me*. At the heart of these accounts is his unwavering trust in God's marvelous goodness. 'Can there be anything more consoling', he muses in the second of these books, 'than to look at a burden or a humiliation not just as it is in itself, but as the will of God entrusted to you at that moment?'

Embracing Life

In his spirituality, Ciszek rejects any kind of otherworldly piousness, insisting on the connection between the mysterious unfolding of God's wonderful plan and the events of our daily lives. The conviction that God is concerned for us at each moment of our lives enables us to bridge the gap between belief in an all-loving God and the sense of abandonment we sometimes experience in life. Far from any passive fatalism, Ciszek's way is to embrace life for what it brings and, more importantly, for the meaning that each moment can possess. Such a transformative approach is a key for unleashing true peace and joy in living, regardless of the circumstances of our lives. The discernment of God's will in the daily events of our lives leads to an active acceptance of his will as he interacts with our world:

> Across that threshold I had been afraid to cross, things suddenly seemed so very simple. There was but one single vision, God, who was all in all; there was but one will that directed all things, God's will. I had only to see it, to discern it in every circumstance in which I found myself, and let myself be ruled by it.

Walter repeatedly had to re-learn the lesson that God was leading him to embrace. In one moving passage, he describes how he finally came to terms with the reality that he did not excel in strength, cleverness or courage. Indeed, the decisive moment of his interior liberation emerged through his eventual acceptance of this reality. He came to acknowledge that he was not immune to failure and to compromise; rather, it was his willingness to begin again that built up his confidence and faithfulness:

> Each victory over discouragement gave an increase in spiritual courage; every success, however fleeting, in finding the hand of God behind all things, made it easier to recapture the sense of his purpose in a new day of seemingly senseless work and hardship and suffering.

In this way, Walter learned to find meaning in his own contribution to the life of the camp, even if it evaded others:

> I knew they couldn't understand why I worked so hard, why I should suffer hunger and hardship, working all day in a half-frozen river or out in a snow-covered forest, standing in line for hours to get extra bread, enduring sleepless nights, putting up with inadequate housing and tattered clothes. It meant nothing to them for me to speak of an apostolate, for me to say that I did it just to be with them, to be available to them under the urging of God's will. And yet that was the truth of it.

An Inclusive Compassion

Walter's compassionate love, concretely practised in the midst of an unimaginably diverse range of challenges, hardships and rejection, is perhaps the most moving part of his witness. It was frequently tested and challenged, mocked and rejected, or simply unnoticed, by those around him. He nevertheless retained a remarkable ability to empathise with people different from him, to see the motivations of others, even those who despised him, from their perspective. He was able to comprehend the hostility of people from different faiths, even those who were fiercely anti-Catholic. He began to pray for his interrogators in prison, 'Not so they would see things my way or come to the truth so that my ordeal would end, but because they, too, were children of God and human beings in need of his blessing and his daily grace'.

He was even moved to pray for Vladimir Lenin, the notorious father of Russian communism, whose manipulation of the masses steered the country from bitterness to ruthless oppression. 'He was a man, after all,' he reminded himself, 'and he may be in need of more prayers than he is getting.' He was also able to distinguish the harshly dehumanising political system he experienced from the people who lived, worked and died there. While pointing out the inherent weakness in the political ideology of the Soviet Union, his praise for certain concrete accomplishments of the people surely must have been exceptional during the cold war. Those who met him after his return to the United States were struck by the depth and endurance of this call to compassion.

In a most passionate way, Ciszek held the people of Russia in his heart throughout his life. This compassion did not diminish, but rather increased with time. 'I grew to love these Russian people as never before', he wrote after more than two decades of living and suffering in the Soviet Union. The greatness of his life was rooted, not in the success of his endeavours, but in his choice to love and serve in whatever conditions he found himself. At the conclusion of his second book, he declared:

> My apostolate to these people, again in the strange and mysterious ways of divine providence, has ended. But I remember them with fondness and sadness; I pray for them daily. I still remember them along with my Russian Christians of Norilsk and Krasnoyarsk, with my fellow prisoners and friends in the labor camps, in my Mass each morning – and I offer up all the prayers, works and sufferings of each day for their eternal salvation and happiness with God.

Our Challenge Today

Walter Ciszek's words remain as much a challenge to us today as they did in his own time. We find ourselves in a period of history in which ethnic, social, political and religious labels are leading to suspicions and generalised judgements, with the ever-present threat of discord and violence which they generate. The challenge for us is to view people as individuals created and sustained by a loving God, believing, as Walter Ciszek did, that even a person reared in an environment hostile to our vision of the world nonetheless shares in the inalienable search for meaning. Every person, Ciszek insists, yearns for a richer and fuller life, seeks a deeper meaning than material rewards can offer, is troubled by the same problems, and is searching for answers. In his view, we are all united in our common humanity, a view as relevant for us today as it was during the Cold War.

If he were alive, Walter Ciszek would hardly recognise the post-Soviet Russia of today. With the collapse of the communist regime, the Soviet Union has broken into independent countries with greater civil freedoms, including the freedom to practise religion. Disenchantment with many aspects of Western ideology has set in, however, and has led to increasing scepticism about the values and practices of western democracy. The future is unclear, but of course it is never possible to predict the future of this – or any – country. Nevertheless, as Fr Ciszek would undoubtedly remind us, that is not what matters most. What matters is that God, who is faithful, has his plans for the people of Russia, and for all nations and people. He will continue to invite his followers to be attentive to these plans as they unfold in the events of everyday life. To those who dare to say 'yes' – however imperfectly – to his plan in the concrete unfolding of their lives, he will grant the inestimable dignity of sharing in God's work in our world. This alone will give meaning to our lives in whatever circumstances we find ourselves.

In one of the earlier episodes of *With God in Russia*, Walter describes how he and his fellow Jesuits found themselves discouraged by the apparent futility of their service in the Soviet city of Teplaya-Gora. And then, he says, it dawned on them:

> God granted us the grace to see the solution to our dilemma, the answer to our temptation. It was the grace quite simply to look at our situation from his viewpoint rather than from ours. It was the grace not to judge our efforts by human standards, or by what we ourselves wanted or expected to happen, but rather according to God's design. It was the grace to understand that our dilemma, our temptation, was of our own making and existed only in our minds; it did not and could not coincide with the real world ordained by God and governed ultimately by his will.

~ 15 ~

Rutilio Grande (1928–77)

Michael O'Sullivan SJ

The material world is for everyone, without borders.
A common table with a tablecloth big enough for
everyone, like this Eucharist. Each one with a seat,
so that each one comes to the table to eat.

– Rutilio Grande

In 1985, the Irish Jesuit Province established a small community
in the Silloge Road flats in Ballymun, on the northern periphery
of Dublin. It was an area where a high degree of socio-economic
deprivation marked the lives of many of the people. The new Jesuit
community was named in honour of Fr Rutilio Grande, a Jesuit
priest who was little known to most people at the time. He is still
not well known. So, who was he?

An Impoverished Community
On 12 March 1977, at around 5 p.m., Rutilio Grande set out from
Aguilares to say Mass in nearby El Paisnal. Aguilares and El
Paisnal are part of the parish of Aguilares in El Salvador, Central
America. Rutilio knew the road well, as El Paisnal was the little
town where he had been born and raised. His father had been the
local mayor a number of times and some of Rutilio's relatives still
lived there. In 1972 Rutilio became parish priest of the combined

area, which encompassed 30,000 inhabitants.

The great majority of the people in El Paisnal were economically poor. They lived in rural areas in very cramped dwellings, without electricity, running water or adequate sanitation. This reflected the national pattern in a country where great tracts of land, owned by a few, were dedicated to the export of produce like sugar, coffee and cotton. Since this form of agriculture was in no way able to absorb the number of people seeking employment, the majority of the peasants could find work for less than half the days available in any one year.

The result was that, while the work in the countryside gave the peasants a small income, in another way it actually added to their poverty. For example, in 1973 the daily consumption of calories per person in this region was 1,683, whereas the minimum necessary for basic living was estimated at 2,200. These workers, forced to produce food for export in a country where most people were battling hunger, were themselves not even reaching minimum subsistence levels.

Liberation Theology

Rutilio was known as the apostle of rural evangelisation. He had formed a team whose approach to pastoral work was inspired by liberation theology. Liberation theology already existed in an incipient form prior to the Second Vatican Council (1962–65) and to the conference of Latin American bishops in Medellín, Colombia (1968), but both of these events gave it considerable impetus in Latin America, where huge numbers of people were both Christian and mired in poverty.

At the Second Vatican Council, the Catholic Church facilitated the rise of liberation theology by speaking of Christian identity in the modern world, especially in the context of those who are poor. It also spoke about the need to read 'the signs of the times' for the sake of historical fidelity to the desires of God for our world. In Latin America, the growing awareness of the plight of the poor was understood theologically as a sign that God was calling and guiding his people to respond to their historical situation.

These developments in consciousness, as well as the optimism of the 1960s, led to a belief in the possibility of real social change. They led the Bishops at Medellín to declare that 'by its own vocation Latin America will undertake its liberation at the cost of whatever sacrifice'. In the eyes of the bishops, the struggle for liberation was a vocation, because it was not simply about seeking to overcome injustice, misery and oppression; it was, more profoundly, about mediating God's salvation in history on the grounds that such realities were sinful.

The emphasis in liberation theology on giving priority to the economically poor was not only about overcoming such sinful oppression; it was also about how such salvific work was to be carried out. Basic Christian communities were to be developed, bringing the economically poor together around the resources of their Christian faith. The poor were to be trusted and encouraged to read social reality, scripture and Church tradition from the perspective of their own experience of poverty. They were also to be empowered to work together in finding ways of transforming their lives. By engaging in this process, the poor were to be instruments in spreading God's universal saving love at work in history. All of this meant that those who had been used to a clerical model of authority, where certain people were presumed to have the right to tell others how to think, feel and act, now had to adapt to a different way, based on dialogue, solidarity, partnership and mutuality.

Growing Conflict

By assuming this approach, Rutilio and his team found themselves in conflict with those who were afraid the peasants would organise themselves effectively, become self-confident and well-informed, and as a result rise up against their suffering and exploitation. These opponents decided to combat the powerful energy that had been released by using the force of death. The three-mile journey from Aguilares to El Paisnal took Rutilio along a dirt road between two fields of sugar cane. Two companions began the journey with him, Manuel, a seventy-two-year-old man, and Nelson, a fourteen-year-old boy who suffered from epilepsy. Forty-nine years old, Rutilio began the journey that would lead him to his tomb.

At one time, Rutilio had suffered terrible doubts about his own worth, doubts that had tortured him for years and had made him hesitate to present himself for priestly ordination as a Jesuit. He had overcome these doubts, however, just as he subsequently overcame the disillusion he experienced when he was dismissed as formator, lecturer and director of social action in the Major Seminary. The authorities had taken this step because he was too outspoken on behalf of the economically poor, and because he refused to reflect a clerical model of the Catholic Church. Not alone in their fears and concerns, the authorities were persuaded more by the voice of caution than by the prophetic faith of Rutilio and those whose concerns he represented.

Appointed parish priest in Aguilares in 1972, Rutilio quickly came into direct conflict with rich and powerful people. He was vulnerable and he knew it. He had been warned that his life was in danger. On the very day he set out to say Mass in El Paisnal, suspicious people had been spotted around the parish. He was also acutely aware of what they had done to Jesus in his day, as he reminded the people in a homily he preached a few weeks before his death:

> If Jesus were to enter through the border … they would detain him. They would take him to many courts and accuse him of being unconstitutional … of being a foreign Jew, of intrigues through exotic and strange ideas. They would crucify him again. Many prefer a Christ with a muzzle on his mouth. Many prefer a Christ made for our own whims and who acts according to our own interests. This is not the Christ of the gospels.

Clearly, Rutilio realised that to be called to be a companion of Christ, in the circumstances of that time in El Salvador, meant running the same risk as the historical Jesus. But Rutilio was not deterred by this realisation. The people would be waiting. He would go to them.

Final Journey

On that final earthly journey, Rutilio stopped his car to give three young children a lift. As he drove off again it became apparent that a pickup truck was following them. Ahead they saw a blue car with California registration plates. The car was stopped and there were men on either side of the road with weapons by their sides. The pickup accelerated and drove up menacingly behind them. Rutilio and his companions were clearly in danger.

One of the men by the side of the road lit a cigarette. This was the signal for murder. The bullets came from both sides as well as from behind. They pierced Rutilio's neck, head, lower back and pelvis. The elderly Manuel, who tried to shield Rutilio, was also killed. The children in the back of the car survived. They were allowed to run away. As they did so, they heard a further shot being fired. It killed young Nelson, who had suffered an epileptic seizure and was unable to escape the car.

Today three small crosses mark the spot along the road where Rutilio and his two companions were killed. Scripture reminds us that to no greater love is possible than to lay down one's life for one's friends *(Jn.15:13)*. Rutilio Grande died for love of God and of some of the poorest people in the world. The three bodies were brought to the church in Paisnal, and if you go there today you will see three slabs on the ground marking their graves. The Jesuits wanted all three to be buried side by side.

A Spate of Murders

At 10.30 p.m. that evening, the new archbishop of San Salvador, Oscar Romero, arrived to say Mass for the three who had been killed. He had known Rutilio for many years, and a large photo of him was hanging in his simple home when I visited in 1991. Cautious and traditional up to that point, Romero was converted by the assassination of Grande to take a consistently daring public stand on behalf of the poor. Three years later during Mass in a cancer hospital, as he held his arms open at the offertory, Romero was fatally shot through the heart and slumped to his death under the large cross hanging above the altar.

The death of Grande and his companions marked the beginning of a spate of murders in El Salvador. Best known among those killed were Jean Donovan, who had studied in Cork a year earlier, and her three missionary companions from the US (1980), and Ignatio Ellacuria and his five Jesuit companions from the University of Central America (1989). That said, countless numbers of so-called ordinary people were also targeted, people like Elba Julia and her daughter Celina, who had taken refuge with the Jesuit community in 1989, but were murdered with them.

All these stories make us aware that it can be dangerous to be an authentic Christian in this world. They can also make it seem that 'the world has escaped from the hands of God', as Rutilio said on one occasion. But the greatest evidence against such appearances is the testimony of those who, like Rutilio, have found themselves so taken over by God's love that they are ready to offer everything in return. Let us never forget Rutilio and his courageous faith, hope and love. And let us be inspired by him to play our part in standing up for and with those whose struggle for faith and justice reflects God's dream for the world.

~ 16 ~

Vicente Cañas (1939–87)

Fergus O'Donoghue SJ

Bliss of heaven: a thousand times I adore you. Tree of uncountable fruits, Hope of the peoples, Pillar of the weak, listen to my prayer.
– Hymn in the Quechua Language of South America

On 16 May 1987, a group of missionaries went to the small jungle hut that was the home of Br Vicente Cañas, a Jesuit whose last radio contact with them had been forty days earlier. They found his body there and realised that he had been murdered soon after sending his final message. Thus ended a remarkable life that began at Albacete, Spain, in October 1939, seven months after the end of the Spanish Civil War.

A Traditional Training

Vicente Cañas – pronounced 'can-yas' – grew up in a country where poverty was widespread and where the experience of intercommunal violence was so recent and so painful that people preferred not to talk about it. The Catholic Church in Spain had suffered much before and during the civil war, so it was very conservative. When young Vicente entered the Society of Jesus as a brother, in 1961, he received a very traditional training. Young Jesuits lived in big communities, always wore long black cassocks and followed a rigid daily timetable.

Vicente wanted broader horizons, however, as he felt that he had a missionary vocation, so he asked to be sent to a mission country. In October 1965, along with another brother, he was given a missionary's crucifix at a special ceremony in Javier Castle, birthplace of St Francis Xavier. He arrived in Brazil in 1966. This meant not only a change of country and continent, but also a change of language, because Vicente had to learn Portuguese, the language which he would use for the rest of his life.

Changing Times

At that time, the Jesuits, like the whole Church, were experiencing upheaval and the excitement of renewal after the Second Vatican Council. The style of Jesuit living was changing, and there was an eagerness for new missions, with an emphasis on social justice and care for marginalised and forgotten people. Vicente embraced these changes enthusiastically!

Jesuits had worked in Latin America since the mid-sixteenth century. They had a tradition of helping the indigenous people in their struggles against exploitation by colonists from Europe. The most famous apostolate on behalf of the American Indians was in the 'Reductions', in what is now Paraguay and northern Argentina. There the Guaraní people were sheltered and protected from slave-raiders and other oppressors. This was so successful that, uniquely in Latin America, Paraguay today gives the indigenous language, Guaraní, official status equal to Spanish. The music composed for the Reductions – both by Jesuits and the local population – is a unique body of work, which is increasingly valued and performed today.

Vicente became fluent in Portuguese. In 1969, he and a Jesuit priest, Fr Antonio Iasi, formed part of a medical team sent to help the Taipunas, an isolated indigenous tribe. This tribe had been almost wiped out by influenza, to which, unlike Brazilians of European ancestry, they had no inherited resistance. The survivors were immunised and moved to a safer place in 1970, but the experience had a profound effect on Vicente. He increased his contact with the isolated peoples and saw that they were endangered not only by Western diseases, but by government indifference and the hostility and greed of newcomers. So, in 1971, Vicente and another Jesuit, Fr Thomas Lisboa, made the first peaceful contact with the Myky people, who later became so fond of Vicente that they named him Kiwxi, which was the name by which all Indians subsequently came to know him.

Living among the Indians

In 1974 Br Vicente and Fr Thomas made the first contact with the Enawene-Nawe people who live deep in the Mato Grosso do Sul, an area between scrubland and rainforest, in south-east Brazil. The following year, Vicente took his final vows as a Jesuit, on the Feast of the Assumption. His dedication to the Society of Jesus was now complete, just as he was devoting himself completely to the Enawene-Name.

The Enawene-Name is one of more than 200 tribes living in the Amazon forest. They live on fish and vegetables, as well as fruit gathered from the rainforest. They do not hunt or eat meat. Their rivers are threatened by the building of dams and their hardwood trees are sought by loggers. Soya farmers cast greedy eyes on their land.

When Brother Vicent finally went to live amongst them, in 1977, the Enawene-Nawe population had fallen to less than 100 (it is now nearly 600). He wanted to help them to secure their territory and to take care of their health. Living amongst them meant a complete change of lifestyle for him, so Vicente allowed his hair and beard to grow, trimmed his hair across his forehead in the Indian style, wore beads around his neck, large wooden rings in his ears and ate only local food. He learned the basics of their language and, as far as he could, took part in their religious rituals, having realised that they had a profound spirituality. Their Yakwa ritual, which lasts for seven months of the year, asks the spirits to protect them and give them food. By living as one of them, Vicente wanted to bring them closer to Christianity. They responded to him, taking him to their hearts. Living with them helped Brother Vicente to deepen his grasp of the Ignatian desire 'to find God in all things'.

Respect for their Culture

Living in a way that was completely different in appearance and setting from his early Jesuit formation, Brother Vicente was grounded in the Jesuit charism. His ability to adapt showed the basic strength of his Jesuit formation. He was out of direct contact with his fellow Jesuits for months on end, but he felt close to them and was supported by them. The casual outside observer would have seen Vicente as an eccentric European, but those who wanted to exploit Indian land, trees and resources – without any regard for the indigenous people who lived there – regarded him as a meddler and a threat. In their eyes, he defended the Indians too well.

Frequently, religious orders had worked with Latin American Indians not only to convert them to Christianity, but also to Western lifestyles, whilst disregarding their native culture. This began to change in the 1960s, when some missionaries in Latin America reformulated their approach and realised that work with remote and untouched Indians should begin with an understanding of their world view and with a study of their spirituality, particularly their way of relating to creation. All those peoples are deeply religious, it was accepted, so their religious practices should be understood and adapted rather than discarded.

As his fellow-Jesuit, Fr Matias Martin Lenz, recalled in 2010, 'Vicente lived as an Indian with the Indians. He lived with full and consistent solidarity with the Enawene-Nawe people.' When he attended the annual meetings of the regional missionaries from all the religious orders, he spoke of the indigenous people's mysticism and shared his appreciation of it with them. Vicente admired the way that they lived in harmony with their environment.

Jesuits who visited Vicente were amazed at the change in his appearance, because he looked almost exactly like one of the Indians.

A very important Jesuit missionary tradition is called 'inculturation', which means drawing close to unconverted peoples by adopting their lifestyle insofar as this is possible. This Vicente did to a remarkable degree. Only his beard marked him as different, because the local Indians have little facial hair.

Defending their Rights

Vicente helped the people secure the land they needed for fishing and farming. The Brazilian government responded to his lobbying by officially granting the territory for use by the Enawene-Nawe, though the threat of encroachment is always present. This angered, and continues to anger, local ranchers, loggers and soya farmers.

Anthropologists and others put Vicente's work in the broad context of the 'uncontacted tribes' – isolated groups in Latin America and some Asiatic islands who keep away from Western civilization, either from fear of its effects or because they have seen and rejected it. Some of the tribes live very close to western groups who are in contact with them, but they prefer their remoteness. Vicente went to live with the Enawene-Name to help them, because he knew that they would not remain 'uncontacted'. He knew that their future could be assured only by making the authorities aware of their needs and by creating structures to protect them in a huge and land-hungry country.

From 1977, Vicente had added support from another Spanish Jesuit, Fr Bartholomew Melia, who was seven years his senior. Bartholomew had lived in Paraguay since 1954 and became an expert in the Guaraní language, as well as a university lecturer and journal editor. In 1976, he was expelled from Paraguay by the military dictatorship, who were angered because he publicised the systematic killing of the Ache-Guayaki people. He helped in Vicente's work alongside conducting academic research and spreading an appreciation of the Indian cultures of Argentina, Bolivia and Brazil. Bartholomew was deeply impressed by Vicente's apostolic work, realising that he not only looked like an Indian, but thought like the people amongst whom he lived, so there was no pretence or deception in his identification with them. 'Not everybody understood his attitude,' he remarked, 'but [Vicente] abandoned much of himself so that he could respect others in all their differences.' Many years later, Bartholomew was able to return to Paraguay.

A Violent Death

Br Vicente did wonderful work for the Enawene-Nawe people, and that resulted in his murder. As he was loading his boat to make a trip to the nearest Indian village on 5 April 1987, he told his fellow missionaries by radio about his plans. Shortly after that, it seems, somebody entered his hut and stabbed him to death. Vicente had struggled against his killers, but he had no chance. He died violently, surrounded by enemies, without any help or comfort in his final moments. When his body was found, on 16 May, it had dried out, but not decayed. Vicente was buried there, early on the morning of 21 May. His body was covered with a fishing net, according to the Indian custom. The Enawene-Nawe, Rikbatsa and Myky peoples helped to bury him.

Six men, including the local police chief, were eventually named as suspects in Vicente's murder. Two died before the trial began in October 2006 and one was considered too old to stand trial. The case has never been concluded.

Br Vicente Cañas is one of many Catholic martyrs who have died because they supported the poor and marginalised in Brazil, including Fr John Bosco Penido Burnier SJ, who was shot by Brazilian police in 1977, and American Sr Dorothy Stang, who was murdered in 2005. Few of the killers have been brought to justice.

Their work continues.

ABOUT THE CONTRIBUTORS

David John Ayotte

David John Ayotte SJ is currently serving as Parochial Vicar at St Ignatius Parish in Sacramento, California. He leads the Ignatian Spirituality Centre and also oversees the development office. In his past ministries, he served on the faculty at Hekima University College in Nairobi and on the Faculty of Missiology at the Pontifical Gregorian University in Rome. His doctorate is in systematic theology focusing on the thought of Pierre Teilhard de Chardin and globalisation.

Patrick Carberry

Patrick Carberry SJ has served as Rector of Clongowes Wood College, Novice Master for the Irish Jesuits and as Director of Manresa, the Irish province's spirituality centre in Dublin. He has been Editor of *The Sacred Heart Messenger* on two occasions, and he has also been involved in the administration of the Irish province. At present, he is Commissioning Editor for Messenger Publications.

Thomas Casey

Thomas Casey SJ was a professor of philosophy at the Pontifical Gregorian University in Rome from 2002–12. Author of five books and many articles, he has also co-edited (with Justin Taylor SM) *Paul's Jewish Matrix*, a book of specialist articles on St Paul by renowned Christian and Jewish scholars. He is currently Dean of the Faculty of Philosophy in St Patrick's College, Maynooth.

Anthony Corcoran

Anthony Corcoran SJ was born in Tucson, Arizona, and raised in Texas. Having completed his university studies, he joined the Jesuits in the New Orleans province in 1985. Inspired by the writings of Walter Ciszek, he volunteered for the Russian mission and was sent to Siberia after ordination, where he ministered to the local Catholics for twelve years. Since then he has served as Jesuit Superior of the Russian region. Having completed his term, he is currently awaiting his next assignment within the region.

James Corkery

James Corkery SJ taught systematic theology at the Milltown Institute of Theology and Philosophy in Dublin for more than twenty years. He is author of *Joseph Ratzinger's Theological Ideas: Wise Cautions and Legitimate Hopes* and has co-edited, with Thomas Worcester SJ, a collection of essays entitled *The Papacy Since 1500: From Italian Prince to Universal Pastor.* Since 2014 he has been a member of the Faculty of Theology at the Pontifical Gregorian University in Rome, where he teaches fundamental and dogmatic theology. He has also been active in the ministry of spiritual accompaniment and in directing the Spiritual Exercises of St Ignatius.

Philip Fogarty

Philip Fogarty SJ spent many years in the ministry of education, particularly as Headmaster of Clongowes Wood College, Co Kildare, and later as Headmaster of Coláiste Iognáid, Galway. He subsequently served as assistant to the Irish Jesuit Provincial. Author of many books and article, he is currently living in the US, where he continues to write and where he also directs retreats and offers spiritual direction, particularly in the Pittsburg diocese.

David Gaffney

Not long after ordination, David Gaffney SJ responded to the formal call of the Irish Jesuits to make marriage and the family apostolate their next priority after education. He devotes himself to the traditional parish visitation of families, both as a way of focusing on this apostolate and as a means of building community for a minority Church. He writes a weekly syndicated column in a regional daily newspaper, often featuring family issues.

Brian Grogan

Brian Grogan SJ is a former President of the Milltown Institute of Theology and Philosophy in Dublin, where he was Associate Professor of Spirituality. He works and writes on Ignatian Spirituality and is the author of *Reflective Living, Love Beyond All Telling, Finding God in All Things, Our Graced Life-Stories* and *God You Are Breaking my Heart*, all published by Messenger Publications. Amongst his other books and articles is *Alone and on Foot: Ignatius of Loyola*, which was published by Veritas in 2008.

Peter Knox

Peter Knox SJ was born in Johannesburg. Following his initial university studies, he joined the Jesuits in 1983. While working in a parish in Soweto, he was privileged to welcome Nelson Mandela home upon his release from prison. Following assignments in student chaplaincy and in the Jesuit Institute in South Africa, he completed his doctoral studies in Aids, Salvation and traditional African religion. He teaches theology in Hekima College, Nairobi, where he is also deputy principal and dean of the Jesuit School of Theology. He is particularly interested in environmental ethics and Pope Francis's encyclical *Laudato Si'*.

Fergus O'Donoghue

Fergus O'Donoghue SJ is a Dubliner, who studied history at University College Dublin, before entering the Society of Jesus in 1970. After ordination, he went to Catholic University in Washington, DC, for studies in Church history. Fr O'Donoghue taught in Dublin, at the Milltown Institute of Theology and Philosophy, where he was also Librarian. For ten years, he edited *Studies*, the Irish Jesuit quarterly review. He now works at St Francis Xavier Church, Gardiner Street, Dublin.

Kevin O'Higgins

Kevin O'Higgins SJ is an Irish Jesuit who spent many years working in Paraguay. He still retains a strong interest in all things to do with

Latin American. His main activity over the past thirty years has been teaching philosophy. He is now Director of the Jesuit University Support and Training (JUST) project in Ballymun, Dublin, which offers personal and academic support to people from the area who wish to pursue university-level studies.

Michael O'Sullivan

Michael O'Sullivan SJ, an Irish Jesuit priest, has lived and worked in Latin America, including El Salvador. He has specialised in liberation theology and spirituality. He is Executive Director of the Spirituality Institute for Research and Education in Dublin (SpIRE), is Programme Leader of the MA in Applied Spirituality in Waterford Institute of Technology, and is Research Fellow at the University of the Free State, South Africa.

David Stewart

A native of Scotland and member of the British province, David Stewart SJ has worked at various times in secondary education, chaplaincy and young adult ministry. He has been superior of an international Jesuit community of scholastics in London, and is currently London correspondent for the US Jesuits' magazine, *America*. At present, he is Director for England and Wales of the Pope's Worldwide Prayer Network, formerly known as the Apostleship of Prayer.

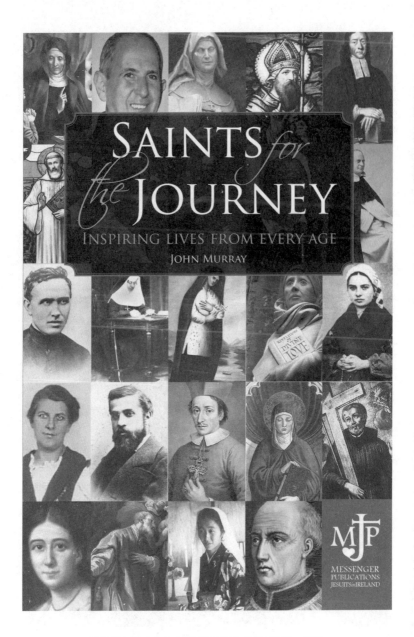

SAINTS for the JOURNEY

INSPIRING LIVES FROM EVERY AGE

JOHN MURRAY

MESSENGER
PUBLICATIONS
JESUITS in IRELAND

WWW.MESSENGER.IE

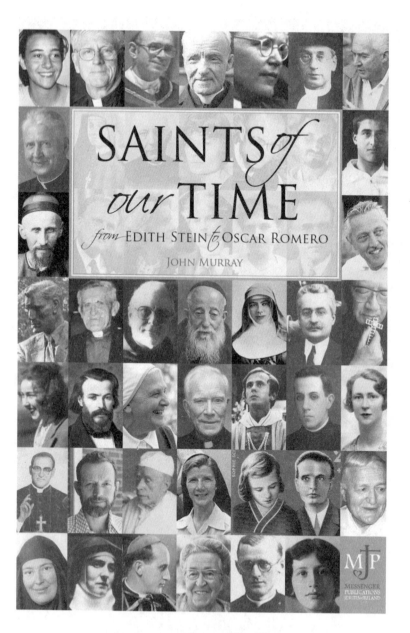

SAINTS of our TIME

from Edith Stein to Oscar Romero

JOHN MURRAY

MESSENGER
PUBLICATIONS
(JESUITS in IRELAND)